Sea Kayaking
From Mountains To Ocean

Reflections on watershed ecology
in the Washington Pacific Northwest

Dan Baharav

Murrelet Publishing
Bellingham, Washington

Library of Congress Cataloging-in-Publication Data
Dan Baharav, 1940
    Sea kayaking from mountains to ocean: reflections on watershed ecology in the Washington Pacific Northwest / by Dan Baharav.

    p. cm.
    LCCN 2009933979
    ISBN-13: 978-0-9825326-0-7
    ISBN-10: 0-9825326-0-1

    1. Watershed ecology - Washington - Pacific Coast. 2. Watershed ecology - Washington (State) - San Juan Islands. 3. Natural history - Washington - Pacific Coast. 4. Natural history - Washington (State) - San Juan Islands. 5. Sea kayaking - Washington - Pacific Coast. 6. Sea kayaking - Washington (State) - San Juan Islands. 7. Pacific Coast (Wash.) - Description and travel. 8. San Juan Islands (Wash.) - Description and travel.
    I. Title.

    QH105.W2B34 2010   577.5'1'09797
                 QB109-600143

All photographs by the author.

Edited by Eva Baharav
Book Design, prepress and map by Kathleen R. Weisel
Cover by Dan Baharav

Published by
Murrelet Publishing
Bellingham, Washington

Printed in Hong Kong

Front cover: Baker Lake with Mount Shuksan in the distance.
Back cover: Sea kayaking in the Strait of Juan de Fuca.

For Eva

This book is about sea kayaking the waters east and west of Interstate 5 from the Canadian border in the north to Olympia in the south.

Contents

The sea kayak is one of the simplest vehicles crafted to negotiate rivers, lakes, and oceans.

Prologue

It's a beautiful Mediterranean summer morning in 1942. I am two, sitting in a stroller, being pushed by my mother along Dizingoff Street in Tel Aviv. At the corner of Keren-Kayemet Boulevard my mother stops and turns around to chat with a friend. As the conversation with the friend gets more involved, I get bored, climb out of the stroller, and, arms stretched to reach the handle bar, I quietly trot the stroller away along the boulevard sidewalk. Crossing the busy Ben-Yehuda Street I continue my stroller-pushing march, hands barely touching the handlebar, toward Gordon Beach. A young woman, standing by the doorstep to her little whitewashed house overlooking the many steps leading to the popular beach down below, asks me where my mother is. My reply doesn't make much sense to her so she invites me to her house for a glass of juice, and hurries to inform the police. Meanwhile my mother, in total panic, unable to believe that I could have disappeared so fast, is running up and down the streets looking for me. Two hours and two policemen later she finds me in the woman's house sitting on a high chair, drinking juice, looking through the window at the crisp Mediterranean blue waters and the gentle waves surging the shoreline.

This was my first solo expedition to the seas.

Going solo is my thing.

Although I am a social person, have been happily married for four and a half decades, love my children and grandchildren, and readily share company with other people, when I roam in nature I definitely live up to the old cliché "Two is one too many". I like to contemplate the wilderness, from a kayak cockpit or on foot alone. I like to leave the crowd behind me. Solo kayaking allows me to explore vast areas on my own terms, my own agendas, and my own wishes. I like moving through vibrating seas, lakes, and rivers. This is why I go there so often. I also like simplicity. Sea kayaking is one of the simplest vehicles crafted to negotiate calm or storm waters.

Sea kayaking, like many outdoor activities, requires careful planning for preparation, execution, and return. It starts with the proper equipment and clothing and then demands skill and experience. I gained skill by hours of paddling in various conditions, by practicing wet exits, wet entries, and rolls, by studying weather, by learning to understand the water. Whether going out for a one hour exercise or for a several week expedition, providing for basic safety, and reliable equipment and clothing, is the same. I prepare myself for the worst each time I think of going out to the water. I spend about five hours of planning for each hour of paddling. I study routes on topographical and nautical maps for hours, draw navigational lines and numbers, study tides, ripples, and currents. For me this is as fun as the actual paddle. Then comes the moment of truth: the moment when I sit in the cockpit all geared up and shove off for the water. Many a time I paddle leisurely and reflect, but at other moments I sit tight and focus when conditions on the route get to be unpredictable and treacherous, and keen judgment of the situation is being called for. My rule is to never push myself beyond my limits. At times "calculated risks" are taken but they are always within the scope of my abilities. When I finally come back ashore I routinely take the time to carefully attend to the gear and the clothing. I look at the unpacking routine as the preparation for my next trip.

Interstate 5 is a massive north-to-south human corridor slicing into the heart of the state of Washington's wetlands. Massive human development within the I-5 corridor is the vector of industrial and agricultural pollutants to the Puget Sound and then to the Pacific Ocean.

Hydro-electric structures dam the rivers' natural flow and miles of power lines connect the energy needed for the fast urban growth.

The Pacific Northwest is beautiful, particularly in Washington: it is green and lush. For a sea kayaker it is Eden. Wilderness can be found just outside one's doorstep. The mega-freeway, the Interstate 5 corridor, links people with a vast array of green parks intertwined by navigable streams, rivers, lakes, and inlets all connected to the Pacific Ocean in close proximity. Although the air distance between the Cascades uplift and the ocean shoreline is relatively short, on a spatial-temporal scale it is vast. From an ecological perspective, this geography is magnificent, diverse, and wild and I felt a strong urge to traverse its myriad elaborate watersheds and drift with its water courses to the ocean. I wanted to explore nature through the realm of the watershed: its features, its patterns and its continuum with the sea, drifting with the water flow to have a grasp on the watershed's power and direction.

But I also had an agenda.

The Interstate 5 corridor is in the midst of drastic ecological changes. People are exerting major environmental influences through their self-serving interests. Interstate 5 links people to undeveloped open spaces privately and publicly owned. Access roads are cut into the forest; Bridges are constructed to cross streams and rivers; Subdivisions replace wetlands and farms; Hydro-electric structures dam the rivers' natural flow; Forests are cut for timber; Rivers, estuaries and seas are heavily used for fisheries. All these activities, to name a few, compete with the vital setting of our natural environment.

When asked about current global environmental problems some people are concerned with population growth, arguing that our current level of environmental exploitation cannot be sustained. Others reason that further economic growth is inevitable and profoundly desirable. The former firmly advocate halting the decline by changing human ways of life, while the latter reason that there is an over exaggeration about the current processes of environmental degradation and advocate to maintain the environmental status quo. I will argue that people fundamentally believe that the present environmental issues call for conservation, but are reluctant to take action when these issues conflict with their own immediate needs. In his recent book, *Collapse*, Jared Diamond asks: "Will modern technology solve our problems, or is it creating new problems faster than it solves old ones?"

By kayaking these Cascadian avenues along their courses to the ocean I wanted to contemplate the details of these watersheds: Are we doing fine or are we on the road to collapse?

I am a professional field ecologist experienced in the biogeography and ecosystem communities of various landscapes from tundra to desert to ocean. I hike, I paddle, and I climb. I have been doing this for five decades now in academia, government, and various private sectors. This book is about my contact with the landscape I now live in and my feelings and reflections on its ecology. But it also contains my reflections on ecology and conservation anywhere on the planet. It is about solitude and contentment and gratification. It is about fun, sea kayaking, and reflections on natural history, expressed in stories and photographs.

This book is not a guide. The daily trips cover long mileage; they can be segmented if desired so one can camp along the routes. Maps (topographical and nautical) can be easily found elsewhere and there are numerous excellent books describing some of the routes for specific information along the North Cascades rivers, Puget Sound, and the Pacific Coast.

Traveling in a kayak opens avenues for exploration, fishing, photography, relaxation, and solitude. An encounter with wildlife is always a thrill.

On the way from the Cascades headwaters to the open Pacific Ocean.

ONE

North Cascades Watersheds – Puget Sound

The North Cascades uplift is rugged and bold. Some parts of the watershed lands are controlled by private timber companies and some parts are controlled by public agencies. Excessive timber removal causes slope erosion and deterioration of the local biota.

14

The headwaters of the Nooksack River are within the Mount Baker and Mount Shuksan glaciers.

1

Nooksack River and Delta

Coleman Glacier, between Black Buttes and Mount Baker summit. The massive Glacier has recently dwindled in size due to rising temperatures in the Northern Cascades.

The Nooksack River drainage avenues water from the Mount Shuksan and Mount Baker glaciers all the way into the north tip of the Puget Sound where it creates an enormous shallow and dynamic delta. The cold, fast-running main course gulps rushing water near Deming from its two main tributaries: the North and South Forks. The river is wide with extensive beaches, sand bars, and large and small islands, and runs swiftly year round. The diverse vegetation along the marshy banks blocks and isolates the river course from the much developed urban and farming communities through which it passes.

The dense plant configurations along the Nooksack maintain a dynamic and vital ecological corridor connecting foothill and

Dakota Creek empties its waters into Drayton Harbor just off Interstate 5 at the United States border with Canada. The daily tidal changes are remarkable at the estuary sections of the river. Together with its neighboring California Creek, the two rivers are lovely for exploring abundant and diverse waterfowl.

16

mountain habitats with the ocean's Puget Sound. An enormous bulk of organic matter, both live and decayed, passes through this grand watershed, nurturing both young and adult forms of life. It is habitat to waterfowl species, raptors, song and ground birds, and small and large mammals all of which share this corridor in a massive, vibrant web of life. The river is a main course for various salmon fish providing spots for spawning and nursing along its tributaries. During the winter months floods are common and the river flashes in great speed, sometimes exceeding nine-ten miles per hour, carrying large fallen trees and tangled snags. This is when sea kayakers should stay out of it. But

during summer and fall, when the river is low, it is a great river to sea kayak along its negotiable course, from east of Saxon all the way to its mouth, some sixty miles west.

On a mid September morning, partly cloudy and cool, I rolled my kayak into the Nooksack River just west of hwy 544 in Everson River Park where access is easy. The river water level was low at this time of the year flowing through a narrow channel deep enough to paddle at ease. The color of the water was deep green with some pale blue touches at the shallows. The water was cold and the flow was moderate. My plan was to paddle all the way to the river's delta, some 30 miles downstream and then continue

Mount Baker stands tall above the Nooksack valley floor with its productive and flourishing farming lands.

for another two miles in Bellingham Bay to the take-out at Squalicum Beach Park in Bellingham. I timed my course so that the entrance into the delta will take place at high tide predicted to be 8.5 feet in seven hours. The Nooksack Delta area is not recommended for paddling if the tide is less than six feet; at low water levels the shallows become mud flats. Although the flats are packed with diverse sea birds, getting stuck in the mud means at least five hours of camping in your kayak before any stirring is feasible. With this time table in mind I needed to paddle at six miles an hour on average, including rests, explorations, and dealing with obstacles. I estimated the river flow at its deep negotiable sections to be about four miles an hour all of which translated to an easy pace requiring little effort on my part.

The first three miles were fast and smooth and I was gliding through the main passages with ease. Throughout most of this section the river bottom was visible through the transparent green-blue water. Few chum salmon swimming upriver were visible alongside the kayak in the deeper sections. It seemed that immersing a simple hand net in the water while floating would have most likely resulted in a catch. In places I halted my kayak just to observe the fish in their pursuit up the river, contemplating how our paths were intersecting with the salmon going upriver, and me going downriver. Salmon exemplify a group of organisms that need one continuous, uninterrupted corridor from the open sea to the river headwaters for their spawning and rearing habitats. Lately, increasing human development along the Nooksack river banks has led to the fragmentation of this continuity.

I continued my paddling and at a narrow passage, just west of mile two, a noisy racket drew my attention: a group of seven turkey vultures and three mew gulls were busy feeding on some fish carcasses. Ignoring my presence as I lingered at a sand bar a few yards away, the small gulls hovered over the vultures screeching at the top of their voice while threatening to steal some morsels of food. The turkey vultures, not threatened in the least, rebuted by menacingly spreading their wings, which proved

to be quite effective. I continued paddling thinking of how these birds, common in this area throughout the summer and fall, are dependent on the salmon and other fish for their livelihood, when I started decelerating as I was meandering at sharp angles along the river course at mile four. Stacked stems, hanging dry branches, and exposed rocks, had to be negotiated in and around the deeper channel. Ecologically, these natural obstacles are safe havens for diverse organisms, but for me they presented challenging maneuvers.

More clouds rolled in from the west shrouding the sun momentarily illuminating everything on a silvery aura. I turned my head briefly to catch a glimpse of magnificent Mount Baker, behind my back, standing tall and impressive enveloped in several tones of blue. Although the river course drew my constant attention, the float was magnificent. I slowed down by a jet boat to chat with two guys fishing.

"Any luck yet?" So far their efforts led to naught; they just settled in.

Alongside a sand bar by a deep channel further down, I met two other fishermen in their boats. No trophy either. These guys had some doubts about their likelihood of catching any salmon; they haven't noticed any fish movements as of yet. I shared with them my observations thus far and they returned big smiles. They definitely seemed as happy as I was, just being on the river in such a beautiful setting. Apparently

The Nooksack River estuary is an extensive ecological marvel. It has several outlets into Bellingham Bay, all conveying through high water floodplains with dense woody vegetation.

the chum salmon were just beginning to move into the Nooksack having spent three to five years at sea before returning to their natal nooks upriver. Much more massive movements upstream would occur in October and November. On their move upriver the chum prefer the deep section of the channel and since they do not leap off the water they are hard to spot when they are at low densities. The chum salmon is the most abundant salmon species in the state of Washington and according to recent surveys the Nooksack watershed population is healthy. The other sought salmon species in the Nooksack at this time is the chinook. These are double the size of the chum, run in shallower water, and arrive at their spawning spots in September. Lately the chinook population in the Nooksack watershed has shown signs of decline.

Now I passed under the Meridian Street bridge in Lynden about twenty minutes earlier than predicted. The hum of passing cars on the bridge was the first reminder since my launch that I'm actually floating in an urban surrounding. Fortunately the noise subsided immediately after I passed the bridge, when I entered a deep and wide section of the river in a quiet rural setting where shrubs and trees along the banks abound. It was peaceful here. The sound of the rushing water crushing into the colorful

The mouth of the Nooksack River is loaded with drifting wood, gigantic tree stems, and organic deposits.

20

rocky bottom, the sight of the large sandy and gravelly beaches, and the abrupt and bold North Cascade Mountains looming in the distance at each turn filled my lungs with excitement. Paddlers who traveled the Nooksack think that the scenery of Mount Baker and the Cascades here outscale any other river emptying into Puget Sound. I tend to agree with them.

For the next six miles where the river meandered often turning almost at sharp ninety degree turns, I spotted more fishermen. These sections are apparently preferred fishing spots since the shallows and the deeps abut. For me, these sections create navigation dilemmas. Just before each turn the center course of the river is shallower than the channels alongside the banks, requiring a quick split-second decision where to turn. Ripples, small or moderate, signal a "No" zone for the kayak: they announce shallows. In places where the river is running fast those ripples zoom toward the bow forcefully vacuuming the kayak into the shoals which means, most of the time, stepping out of the cockpit and dragging the kayak back into a deeper course.

As I approached the bridge of I-5, a great blue heron soaring low and two ospreys screeching at high pitch crossed my line of travel. I was excited to see those ospreys, knowing that soon they would take off all the way to Central America and the Amazon River and even further south to Chile, where they winter in places close to water and prey. Ospreys are common breeders along the waterways of the I-5 corridor during spring and summer. They are monogamous and pairs repeatedly return to the same nesting site each spring. However, in the autumn, usually in October, the female takes off to her wintering spot, while the male lingers a while longer to assist the young before departing to his separate winter spot. For about a month they travel these long distances solo, refueling as needed en route, to meet again in April at their exact nesting site. I can't begin to think what they tell each other when they meet again after their long journey.

As I continued my journey, the familiar urban humming noise of moving cars again disturbed the early afternoon tranquility. There are actually two bridges for the Interstate, one for each two lane direction. In a way, floating under these monstrous sinister ugly bridges makes you feel elated and exhilarated. Even the river, let alone the kayak, appears minute and diminished in comparison to the mighty bridge pillars, steel, concrete, and noise.

The river is wide and slow where it passes through the town of Ferndale. It was mid afternoon now and I could see pedestrians strolling on the riverfront trail, some with dogs, and some with kids. Adults were fishing along the rocky banks, sea gulls and crows were vociferously fighting

for whatever leftovers were found on the rocks, and a shrieking kingfisher zoomed through the tree branches as I paddled this urban section. For the next three miles I meandered along with the river through the secluded marshy habitat of Tennant Lake State Wildlife Area and finally landed on a small islet for a brief rest in an area with some extended sand bars and sandy shorelines.

A flock of dunlin, eleven in number, landed on a sand bar not far from my kayak. They immediately went into feeding action, moving back and forth, like a marching band, drilling their stout bills into the soft sand right at the muddy area by the waters' edge. I was astounded by the flock's composure. Even though each individual bird looked for its own food item, as I observed more closely, I noticed a synchronized and precise group motion as they were moving about. I was wondering: Isn't it a bit early to see these shorebirds here? They usually do not arrive here from their northern tundra breeding grounds until late in the fall. Perhaps these dunlins stayed here all summer, as they sometimes do.

The time was close to 4 PM when I entered the Nooksack Delta via a narrow outlet off the main river channel alongside Marietta. There are only a few river outlets into Bellingham Bay, all conveying through high water floodplains with dense woody vegetation in the center and grassy tidal mudflats at the edges. The estuary is extensive, and loaded with drifting wood, log gems, and organic debris. Suddenly, the velocity of the water decreased to nil as I entered into the estuary. Some channels were stretched short to dead-end. It was a maze. I had explored the estuary-delta many times before: summers, autumns, winters, and springs. Each time I experienced surprises and changes.

One can explore the inner and outer delta shores for hours, or just zip through any one of the three connecting channels. Exploring the nine outer toe-like grassy bars and their inlets from Fish Point at the west entrance to Marine Drive bluffs at the east entrance to the river, can be accomplished comfortably at tides higher than six feet. At tides lower than three feet the mudflats extend way into Bellingham Bay.

I was now about quarter of a mile from the mouth of the river where Bellingham Bay opens up, and could see Mount Baker and The Sisters shining in the distance just hanging over the city of Bellingham in glory. At the mouth of the river the piles of gigantic tree stems and branches which the Nooksack had been depositing there for years were partly covered with water: a good sign that the area was still flooded. A flock of great blue herons was perched on a few of the oddly shaped log gems in front of me. Hundreds of sea gulls and various species of ducks surrounded the water. A lone bald eagle landed on top of a massive partly submerged log. As I approached

the herons, they took off to a nearby stem, soaring low, making a large circle above my head, blasting their familiar cranky calls.

The river mouth to the bay, on both sides, is loaded with gigantic wood piles of astonishing sizes and shapes. Diverse bird species usually abound here: great blue herons, shorebirds, wading and diving ducks, grebes, gulls, ospreys, and bald eagles looking for assorted prey. River otters, harbor seals, and California and Steller sea lions are also part of the local animal checklist. Going slowly with the kayak, keeping distance from the birds with extended stops for observation, I looked for mammals searching the river mouth area and the estuary for fish, but couldn't find any today.

The delta holds the assemblage of life dispersed along the Nooksack watershed. It is a core ecological system: it is a terminal for organic matter moved along the river and its tributaries, maintaining an array of life so vital to human existence. It is what we should strive to preserve.

It was close to sunset. The shifting colors of the moving high clouds were stupendous. I could stay here within the Nooksack River mouth forever exploring the shallows, shooting photos and watching the animals and the scattered wood sculptures.

As the darkening night unfolded I turned the bow toward Squalicum Beach two nautical miles in the distance, paddling quietly, gazing at the fading glaciated Mount Baker.

Sunsets are mesmerizing in the Nooksack Delta. The long summer evenings turn sea kayaking in the river's outlets into an exquisite pleasure.

24

Lake Whatcom is nestled between the Nooksack River watershed in the north and the Samish River watershed in the south. The lake is the source of drinking water for the city of Bellingham and surrounding towns and farming communities. High density residential development and recreational activities along its shores have recently altered the water chemistry of the lake, raising concerns for its biological health.

Skagit River and Delta

The Skagit River east of Rockport is swift and scenic. Glacial icy waters rush into its main artery from nearby tributaries enriching the river with organic matter to support a wealth of organisms along its lengthy course.

The Skagit River collects its waters from a gigantic geographical spectrum. Hundreds of tributaries—as far north to the Skagit Range in British Columbia, as far east to the Northern Cascades at Washington Pass along Washington Highway 20, and as far south to Glacier Peak Wilderness—make their way to this river's main artery west of Ross Lake.

The Skagit River watershed and its basin are the largest and most impressive in the Northern Cascades. Building in size and flow magnitude, it meanders west disembouguing into an elaborate delta just southwest of Mount Vernon, Washington.

Tons of organic matter move through the watershed's steep canyons, cascading streams, rivers, marshes, and large prolific valleys. The complex riparian communities building the Skagit water course with their myriad channels of creeks and streams of various sizes support the largest populations of salmon spawning in the Northern Cascades. These include all five native salmon species: the chinook, chum, coho, pink, and sockeye, in addition to healthy steelheads and cutthroat trout.

Starting in early fall, these anadromous species swim vigorously from the Puget Sound up into the Skagit River to their familiar nests. This impressive salmon migration, especially of chums and coho, invites a large number of bald eagles to maintain a winter-long feast. Starting in mid November, bald eagles convene at the upper Skagit River, alongside Highway 20, and by January they are seen in large numbers perching on trees and logs close to the water line, trotting on sand bars, or soaring over the area, especially between the towns of Marblemount and Rockport.

Because of this river's enormity, I decided to kayak the Skagit River in three segments, each offering a different perspective: the upper river, the Baker Lake area, and the lower river and its vast array of estuaries opening into the Puget Sound.

On a sunny winter morning in early January, I entered the Skagit River at the town of Marblemount under the bridge of Cascade River Road that leads to Highway 20. The air was chilly and the water cold, green, and swift. Coming up here this morning I noticed a large group of bald eagles active along the sand bars between Rocky Creek and Illabot Creek. I was hoping that the high swift water would not hamper my attempts to observe and photograph the feeding eagles. With these thoughts I took off into the swift current.

The water was fairly fast but flowing smoothly, and I settled my legs comfortably in the cockpit, stretching my torso while holding the paddle horizontally, to make sure that the lengthy kayak is under control. Before I had a chance to orient myself properly, the noisy water of the Cascade River rushed in from my port. Immediately west and south where the two rivers meet, the Skagit curved sharply to the north for about 200 yards and then turned sharply again to the west to reveal a spectacular view of the fresh snow-covered Cascade Range with its precipitous cliffs and lacerated peaks. The coniferous green slopes were all clothed in snow garniture with the leafless twigs of the riverbank shrubbery completing the wintry scene under amazingly crisp blue skies.

A lone great blue heron was resting silently at the edge of a small sand bar covered with dead fall and wintering shrubs paying no attention to my passing nearby.

As I crossed the Corkindale Creek entrance, I saw two bald eagles soaring low in front directing my gaze towards the distance where I could see on an expansive sand bar, a number of eagles, some perched on a convoluted snag, some on dry stems

Numerous cascades snake down from the jagged ridges of the Northern Cascades into the Upper Skagit River during snow and ice meltdown in the spring months.

Bald eagles in large numbers forage the Skagit River waters for salmon.

28

alongside it, and some rambling on the soft sand. I figured it was a good time to slow down my pace. As I got closer to the group I located a spot on a shore south of the sand bar and decelerated my kayak anchoring a distance from the raptors—eleven in number—who didn't appear to notice me while I was stealthily tinkering with my camera. Four individuals on the ground were searching for something close to the water line. Even though I could not see any salmon or fish remains in the vicinity, I knew they must have been looking for them, as this would be their favorite food this time of year.

These raptors, often solitary, can become gregarious during fall and winter when they form communal day perches and night roosts along river banks. In the spring, loyal to their nesting site, mature pairs mated for life will increase their demands for food to nourish their two-to-three fast growing eaglets. At this time their menu includes a diverse array of small and medium sized live animals and occasional carrion. The eagle— endemic to North America—was officially declared the national emblem by the US Continental Congress in 1782 as a living symbol for space and freedom. In 1973, due to its declining numbers consequent

The Skagit River below the town of Concrete.

to habitat loss, the eagle was entered into the endangered species list. However, bald eagle numbers are now on the rise, and in 2007 this raptor has been delisted from this status in the lower 48 states.

I observed the eagles for a while and then floated on down the river. More eagles were perching along the river banks, seemingly relaxed, as I moved fast past the town of Rockport passing four fishing boats and a group of noisy rafters. As I was meandering with the Skagit River toward my take-out beach at Rasar State Park south of the town of Concrete, I was thinking of the pair of bald eagles terrorizing the waterfowl

where we reside. We live on Lake Louise, a tiny lake on the outskirts of Bellingham, Washington. The lake is surrounded by tall Douglas fir, red cedar, and hemlock trees and myriad deciduous trees and shrubs. The south and north sections of the lake are shallow and marshy, managed by a group of beavers. The lake is highly productive enabling diverse animal life year around. Geese and ducks are especially fond of the lake's habitats and pairs are nesting there year after year.

Life had been quiet and peaceful until the early summer of 2007 when a pair of bald eagles nesting in the vicinity started marauding and plundering every duckling, gosling, baby marten and baby mink in sight to feed their eaglets. Inasmuch as my wife and I could not overcome the sadness of the slow disappearance of the personally named "babies" we had been watching hatching out of their nests, we had to come to terms with this inevitable cycle of life where each species supports the life of all other species in this endless recycling web of life. So it is with the salmon and the eagles in the Skagit. On this note I pulled out of the water, happy to have had the opportunity to see the eagles from water level.

Baker Lake, which is part of the Skagit river watershed, is about ten miles long nestled within the shadows of the Mount Baker and Mount Shuksan glaciers. The east side of the lake features giant western red cedars and Douglas firs, some of the largest in the Pacific Northwest. The enclosed jagged ridges and glaciated valleys receive more than 120 inches of rainfall annually. The huge evergreen and deciduous trees and the lush understory are remarkable.

On a cool morning in the spring I set my kayak at the lake's northwest tip near Shannon Creek. My plan was to circumnavigate the lake clockwise—an eighteen to twenty mile paddle—and to visit one of the largest cedar trees in the northwest, located on the east side of the lake.

The slopes hugging the waterline were still covered with light snow, especially on the north-facing terrain. The morning was just perfect, with cloudless bright blue skies and a light southeast wind creating crisp shiny gently whispering wavelets. The water was quite cold, but that did not deter a group of ducks from their vigorous activities at the northeast tip of the lake close to the shallows of the delta area created by the rushing water of Baker River. So I pointed the bow toward that corner and paddled swiftly, skirting the water as I gained distance.

It was very quiet and peaceful; no boats or people were visible. The rugged slopes, the sheer-walled cliffs, the glaciers, the water, filled me with joy. The numerous glaciers appeared very close, with Mount Blum and Hagan Mountain just two miles away, Mount Shuksan and its pinnacles and glaciers just five miles directly north of me, and the larger glaciers of Challenger Mountain and Mount Fury about twelve miles further north. I could hear the water cascading down the many creeks that fill the lake.

At the delta, where the melting glacier waters turn murky and gray in color I could count 14 ducks moving along the loud cascading waters. In the shallow waters, sliding the kayak alongside two giant tree trunks looming out of the mud, I watched the birds: some gadwalls busy dabbling, and some common mergansers diving and splashing having their time of day.

Paddling slowly within this serene and beautifully set corner I was contemplating

Baker Lake is cradled between Mount Baker and Mount Shuksan glaciers. The lake is part of the Skagit River watershed.

the grandeur of the Baker River, the main contributor of water draining into this basin. It is large and impressive and waters from all of its tributary system travel downstream into the Skagit River. Kayaking this stretch of the basin, witnessing the magnitude of this vast watershed filled me with awe.

An attempt to slide the kayak into what looked like an open passage with some rocky shoreline extending into a dense marshy habitat about a mile wide got me nowhere, it was too shallow and rocky. In my attempts to maneuver, I scared a pair of gadwalls that took off like bullets twenty yards in front of me from a dense shrubby insert. I backed off into more navigable space and continued along the east shore of the delta. To my starboard I could see Mount Baker with its entire magnificent snowy cone standing tall and impressive.

Boulder Glacier just below the peak was glaring in the radiating sun, and to the left I could see Sherman Peak illuminated with myriad pastel colors. The scene was serene and almost unreal. I could stay here all day, and probably should have. But I had reason to move on, and at the mouth of Noisy Creek I pulled into a small sandy spit and beached the boat. A few months earlier I had met three kayakers from Bellingham near Shannon Creek who told me that one of the largest, if not the largest, red cedars in the Northwest can be found not more than half a mile up the east shore trail from the bridge crossing Noisy Creek.

Bushwalking alongside the rushing creek I located the Baker Lake Trail and headed north, crossing the bridge of Noisy Creek and perhaps 300 yards further on, I found the unmarked narrow trail going southeast. The trail meanders among enormous western red cedars, western hemlocks, and Douglas firs, sun-reaching big leaf maples and red alders, diverse fern species, mosses hanging from trees, thickets of lichens and fungi on dead fallen trees and on the ground, all with a dense shrubby understory—a true old growth temperate rain forest. I was within hearing distance from the tumbling waters of Noisy Creek. The trail grade was mostly mild with a few steep stretches.

Suddenly, ten minutes into the trail, there it was, the record size cedar. There was no mistaking it among the other huge trees around as it abuts the trail. I sat by the giant trunk measuring its size with my eyes. The tree is so big that the top cannot be seen. Trying to take a digital picture was hopeless as the tree is too big for the frame.

I learned that this area of the creek had been secured a few years ago from logging as a conservation wilderness unit to maintain the ecological integrity of the Noisy Creek habitat by leaving it as natural as possible. This Nature Conservancy section is part of the area's habitat continuum, maintaining intact the diverse old growth between Beacon Peak and the Mount Watson permanent snowfields and the Baker Lake shoreline.

Sitting alone, quietly, among these humongous trees, listening to the rushing water of Noisy Creek not far in the distance, I was grateful to the admirable individuals who fought successfully the battle for saving this enchanted antiquated forest.

I went back to the kayak and continued south. The wind brushing my face became a little stronger triggered by the late morning warming sun. I paddled close to the eastern shore to take advantage of Mount Baker's glory and at the same time enjoyed watching some of the waterfowl species: the common merganser, hooded merganser, bufflehead, spotted sandpiper, and young gulls, working their way in the shallows where numerous large logged tree stems

The glacial waters of Mount Shuksan cascade their way into Baker River to be stored in Baker Lake. This area is a dream for kayakers who like to hike. Here one can find steep climbing trails, dense temperate rainforests, incredible vistas, ample blueberries and a hot spring hidden in the rugged slopes.

abound—silent remains of the giant trees towering the Baker River basin less than a century ago.

Baker Lake, which is a human-induced reservoir, is fed by the nearby glaciers' runoff. At the mouths of Swift Creek, Park Creek, and Little Park Creek—three rushing creeks plunging from Mount Baker's Park and Rainbow Glaciers—the lake narrows markedly and turns its course directly south. I was meandering among the huge standing stumps, winding my way through this dense ghostly forest. The view to the south, of rolling hills and snow-capped peaks, was magnificent intensified by the absence of people and their numerous activities in and around the lake. This area is crisscrossed by a web of roads, logging, a hydroelectric power station, a fish spawning facility, several boat launches, a resort, and numerous campgrounds—a mess of human-induced impacts.

But right then, as I was listening to the tumbling waters, everything seemed to be perfectly still. The cool spring day, the light breeze, and the spectacular scenery all around, produced one of those rare moments of intimacy with the wilderness surrounding me. "Wilderness" has several biological and social definitions, but for me that particular setting in that particular moment, where I could spend time alone in a vast, diverse and remote ecosystem suited the term "wilderness" perfectly.

Five miles later I reached the Upper Baker Dam. I landed the kayak on a small sandy beach at the northwest cove about 300 yards from the dam. To stretch my legs I climbed to a paved road leading to the dam. I looked down towards Shannon Lake, a reservoir established by the Baker Dam just south and below me, nestled in a huge basin. The view was spectacular.

The hydroelectric power facility at the upper dam was completed in 1959 to meet the increasing demand for electric energy in the Skagit and Whatcom counties' fast growing economy, a mere 35 years after the construction of the lower dam above the town of Concrete. These two dams changed the original ecological pulses of the Baker River riparian habitats, creating a substantial migratory problem for the native Baker

River sockeye salmon which in most likelihood have been using the Baker River basin since the Ice Age. In order to overcome the obstacle for the salmon's upstream-downstream movements created by the towering dams, salmon migration between the two lakes are now successfully being managed by a trap-and-haul system.

Continuing north close to the west shore, I encountered the first other human activity for the day as a power boat zoomed out from Horseshoe Cove. Although the speedy boat was noisy, it did not detract from the magnificent vista of Mount Shuksan to the north and Mount Baker to the northwest. The mid-afternoon sun draped in gold those two mountains and the encircling high forested terrain. For the next few miles this spectacular view accompanied my route. Two ospreys soared above just as I entered the shallow cove created by the Sandy Creek alluvial delta.

As I approached Little Sandy Creek a mile further north, four common loons and a group of common mergansers were busy diving within the bay. I could not take my eyes off Mount Shuksan. It was so beautiful. With Mount Baker and Sherman Peak to my port, and the sun behind me, I could notice almost every crevice and every fold on the Deming, Easton, Squak, Talum, and Boulder Glaciers.

I was paddling at a slow pace now. The wind from the southeast was picking up force, and I decided to land the kayak at the

Baker Lake is a man-made reservoir formed by the impounded waters of Baker River. The huge stems found within the lake and along its shores are a silent reminder of the old forest growth that once hugged the Baker River course.

35

north side of the Boulder Creek entrance to take a short walk. Giant cedar stumps in dense formation populate the shallow soft bottom of the lake and plenty of dead dry wood was scattered on the beach. White-gray melted ice-water was rushing down the creek lending the scenery an intense wild aura.

I laid myself down on the sandy beach, shut my eyes and listened to the rushing noise of the creek, relaxing and enjoying the cool sun. A great blue heron rattled a clapping sound and landed close by forcing my eyes open. A moment later a mature bald eagle placed itself close to the waterline not far from the heron.

I was thinking about the wild habitat I was sharing with these creatures. The modifications made to this place by humans to satisfy increasing demands for drinking water, irrigation operations, and electricity have transformed this place

Baker Lake has transformed the Baker River Basin into a fundamentally different ecological entity in order to cater to the large human demand for water. For now it may look as if in balance with the surrounding natural forest setting. But, is it an illusion?

36

into a fundamentally different ecological system. For a while it may look as if it is in balance with the surrounding natural forest setting, but the consequences in the longer run are totally unpredictable. The adaptive capacity of the new ecological system, with its new trophic level (food chain) make-up, managed by people, is still unknown, in spite of the illusion that all is well.

Even though professional confidence is high in the ability to manage and sustain the biological integrity of the lake, perhaps the task is untenable over time. It is entirely possible that human-induced changes may cause the loss of parts or whole natural elements within the original biological organization and thus degrade its ecological resiliency.

All of a sudden the wind intensified and whitecaps adorned the lake. The narrow bottle-neck stretch, about three quarters of a mile south of Baker Lake Resort, where both banks of the lake are less than half a mile apart, was torrent, loud and bouncy. Because the lake can be nasty at times, I entered quickly into the kayak, and dodging among the stemmed cedars, I rushed out like a missile, taking advantage of the wind and the surge coming from behind. I was paddling around six knots or more making

The entire Skagit River watershed can be observed from the top of Sauk Mountain affording a spectacular 360 degrees vista of the Cascade Mountains and the sea.

sure I'm not too close to the shallows. The lake was now oriented east-northeast, so I had to change course for a while and paddle forty five degrees into the silvery waves to avoid surging waters hitting my port side, until I could direct the bow into the take-out beach just south of Shannon Creek. The final two miles were fast and fun, and landing safely at the beach, where my car was parked, brought to an end the circling of the lake.

Three months later, I was ready to kayak the last segment of the Skagit. My plan was to paddle through the towns of Burlington and Mount Vernon and explore the South Fork section of the Skagit all the way to Skagit Bay, an eighteen mile course. I secured myself into the kayak's cockpit and slid into the Skagit River's swift water at the beach just under the north side of the Highway 9 bridge. I needed to reach my take-out point at the Skagit Recreation Area on the south sloughs of

The Skagit River's enormous delta is haven for thousands of migratory and resident birds. The area is a major winter and spring stopover for snow geese.

38

Fir Island, with a tide level no less than five feet. Therefore timing the course with the tide schedule was crucial. I planned to start at Sedro-Woolley one hour after the maximum high, and then float with the ebb downriver, reaching the town of Conway about four hours before the next maximum high. It was early in the morning, and I was totally engulfed with fog and mist which gave the moment a surreal, almost phantasmagorical, atmosphere, especially with no cars on the bridge. A man wading in the shallows, swinging his fly fishing lure with an elegant rhythmic motion, acknowledged me with a head nod as I slipped by.

This section of the river is wide and vast. I could see in the near distance that the main course meandered along a small island where a group of about 40 swans was grazing close to the waterline. As I paddled by I slowed down to observe them, taking a few photos. A closer look revealed that the group was a mixture of trumpeter and tundra swans. These swans like to winter at this section of the Skagit. They stay here from late fall through May, when they take off to the north.

As I was approaching Nookachamps Creek I spotted another group of about 20 swans grazing in an open field on the south side of the river. The narrow Nookachamps is a major tributary of the Skagit River emptying water from a large basin west of Cultus Mountain. This basin is a rich source for potato and corn growing and is a trove of food for the wintering waterfowl. However, the Nookachamps is also a major carrier of pollutants from farming activities to the Skagit River and then to the delta and to the Puget Sound.

I was now close to the busy section of the I-5 corridor. I could hear the progressive hum of unbroken noise from the passing vehicles drifting along my course. The Skagit is wide here, with a fairly strong current and numerous tree stumps, metal scraps, and other unidentified debris sticking out of the water in front and alongside the kayak creating whirlpools of various sizes around them. I pulled to the middle of the river as it seemed to be the better path along these obstacles. The river turns directly west here under the first bridge connecting Burlington and Mount Vernon. Noise from traffic was intense, especially under the I-5 bridge. This cacophony was in total disharmony with my swift paddling which previously was the only sound I could hear on the river.

Frequent vigorous floods occur within the Skagit River lowlands near Interstate 5 causing recurrent loss, devastation, and grief to local inhabitants who develop too close to the river's banks.

39

In stark contrast with the pristine mountains and glaciers which feed into the Skagit headwaters, human encroachment and massive development in the lower Skagit River water basin chiseled the face of the productive landscape. With former wetlands dried out, riparian vegetation removed, and forests logged, the land was turned into farms, concrete, and malls interspersed with a maze of paved roads, highways and cross bridges.

The altered drainage basin now channels the waters in an accelerated pace resulting in frequent vigorous flood forces that cause recurrent loss, devastation, and grief to local inhabitants. In response, ad hoc expensive flood control measures are implemented, lacking sound conservation consideration.

The immediate need for return on investment leaves no wiggle room for a more deliberate far-sighted set of solutions which will benefit both people and their environment at the same time while maintaining the natural diversity of local ecosystems.

With these reflections, I was now entering the section alongside Mount Vernon town center to relax from the tumultuous I-5 discordant racket. I pulled over into an extensive sandy beach along the west bank by a small city park and wriggled myself out of the kayak for a stretch, a snack, and a recalculation of my navigation time to Skagit Bay. Knowing that maximum high tide at eight feet is around 6 PM, I figured that this height of the water level would give me enough time to explore the estuaries of the sloughs west to Freshwater Slough before landing at the parking area on the banks of Brown Slough.

I reached the Fir Island Road bridge of the South Fork in Conway an hour later and in less than a quarter mile I took the fork into Freshwater Slough. Here the channel which is vegetated with tall cottonwood trees and dense growth of alder becomes narrow and meanders a bit. It was early afternoon and low clouds were drifting slowly into the slough from Skagit Bay as I passed the boat launch of the Skagit Wildlife Area headquarters. This launching site is a favorite kayak and canoe put-in for those who want to explore the delta's waterways. It can be accessed from Conway via Mann Road. I was somewhat surprised at the absence of other floaters.

The current was negligible as it was just after slack time; I expected the rising tide to be at its initial stages by now, although I couldn't detect it yet. In front of me, not more than fifty yards away, a group of mallards and American coots skirted the right bank where it was murky and shallow with opaque green material. The birds have noticed me, but stayed within the shallows. As the coots dove into deeper areas within the shallows, where dabblers can't reach the bottom, surfacing with loads of aquatic plants and small invertebrates for dinner, the dabbing mallards rushed to steal some of the spoils from the coots' mouths. The coots in turn chased the mallards to snatch back some of the plants hanging from the mallards' bills. I was fully entertained to see this game of efficient rummaging and slowed down my paddle, blades hardly touching the water.

Every now and then I inserted the paddle all the way to the river floor to check the depth of the water. It was shallow, less than two feet. I was about a mile from the bay and still could not see the motion of the expected coming flood. I tasted the water for salinity and it was slightly salty. The estuary was apparently slowly filling up with the Puget Sound sea water mixed in.

A hollow grumble of a single great blue heron's take-off was heard across the estuary as I entered into a section of high grass free

40

Extensive arrays of organic matter are deposited within the elaborate tidal marshes of the Skagit delta, providing nutrients and shelter for the many forms of life.

of trees. The giant gray bird glided low into an exposed marshy area covered with dry cattails and gracefully landed in the open water, slowly folding its wings. I looked at its long legs noticing that the water line was reaching the bird's tibial feathers. This was a good sign. It meant that the delta was filling up and that I could now enter the water-covered mud flats with ease. The river was widening now and at last I could see ripples approaching my vessel. As the bow cut through the approaching shiny wavelets, I was overtaken by deep feelings of what solo kayaking means to me: the solitude, the silence, the grandeur of the surrounding waters.

I was now nearing the mouth of the delta. In the distance through the mist I saw hundreds of sea birds broadloom large areas within the flats. The calls of snow geese feeding galore in a nearby field were increasingly growing louder. The Skagit River's enormous delta is haven for thousands of migratory and resident birds that feed in the productive intertidal areas, the lush open fields, and the brushy lowlands. This area is a major winter and spring stopover for the migratory Pacific Flyway.

Estuaries and river deltas are always of great fascination to me. Perhaps it is the beauty of a maze of water and life, maybe it is the dynamics of its energy flow, or both. As an ecologist, I am a student of energy dynamics flowing among ecosystems of varied trophic levels. My doctoral dissertation was on the energy dynamics of a population of an herbivore, a mountain gazelle.

Since then I came to conceptualize natural systems as continuous transformations of energy from producers (plants) through herbivores, carnivores, and omnivores (consumers) to a final decomposition left as detritus starting new cycles of energy transformations. When healthy, estuaries and deltas are among the most productive ecosystems on the planet with energy transformations happening on an intense basis. They are rich in sediments, replete with nutrients, and prolific in both aquatic and terrestrial plants and animals.

The intricate configurations of sloughs and tidal inlets are remarkable for their species richness, their relative abundance, and their energy turnover. Estuaries are governed and energized by the forces of tides. Once isolated from tidal influences, their productive capacity is lost.

The Skagit River estuary is no exception. Extensive arrays of live organic matter and detritus move downriver, deposited as sediments within the elaborate tidal marshes, providing rich nutrients for the many forms of life. Today, as I am exploring some of the channels, meandering along fleets of diverse sea birds, song birds, various raptors, and seals, I wonder whether people will be able to maintain this healthy environment in the face of accelerated growth. Historically, the delta's littoral zone was much more extensive in size than it is today. Man-made dykes, channeling, and draining from the late 1800s and throughout the 1900s to support farming, caused the natural low-tide areas to further recede into the bay.

But this lowland, guarded by a set of high barricaded levees, isolated from the changing tides, is also one of the most productive mixed farming regions in the Northwest. It will take serious well-informed long-term planning to maintain the continued delicate balance between productive man-made environments and productive natural environments.

Continuing in a northwesterly direction, leaving the calls of the snow geese behind, I entered into the Wiley and Dry slough systems where about a dozen harbor seals greeted me. They were so curious that they were popping up close to the kayak, almost touching it with their rounded cute

The Skagit River meets Puget Sound. The mouth of the river is an elaborate delta, with dense vegetation in shallow waters.

heads. From here on through the rest of the evening I had a seal convoy beside me, with the water fairly deep, and the mist changing into light fog, reducing the visibility somewhat.

It was getting late, and it would soon be dark. The bay was flat and still. I enjoyed floating at this dusk hour with the mist and fog rolling low, creating all kinds of unreal, sometimes spooky scenes. The high-tide zone between Dry Slough and Brown Slough was crowded with diving and dabbling ducks busily feeding. Some juvenile sea gulls screeched low above me breaking the silence as I zigzagged my way through the busy animals, readying themselves for nightfall. Slowly I pulled into a grassy take-out site alongside a dyke as a large cloud of snow geese soaring low flew into the night.

44

Trumpeter swans visit the Stillaguamish River delta during winter.

3

Stillaguamish River and Delta

The North Fork Stillaguamish flows swiftly to meet the South Fork Stillaguamish near the town of Arlington to form the main Stillaguamish River that empties into Port Susan, Puget Sound.

Careful contemplation of a topographical map delineating the various watersheds of Mount Baker-Snoqualmie National Forest tracing the headwaters of the Stillaguamish and Snohomish rivers takes you on a fascinating journey into nature's geologic wonders.

Past volcanic eruptions within the high peaks of the Cascades followed by massive downpour of debris and water westward toward the Pacific, embossed terrestrial relief and waterway courses along the way. This is how thirteen thousand years ago the massive eruption of Glacier Peak shaped its western flanks causing the Sauk River with its large watershed to flow into the Skagit River instead of flowing into the Stillaguamish River as it had previously done. Today, the town of Darrington sits at the point of the Sauk River diversion where only a few feet of elevation separate the Stillaguamish and Sauk basins. Here, in Darrington, the Sauk River routes itself impressively northward to Rockport, where it empties into the Skagit River. To the west, just over the hill from there, is the headwater basin for the North Fork of the Stillaguamish River that empties into the main Stillaguamish at Arlington.

Another outcome of those volcanic eruptions is the delineation of the South Fork Stillaguamish and the Pilchuck water courses just west of Granite Falls. Here, at Burn Road flatland, only a few feet separate the two river basins where the South Fork Stillaguamish drains northward to meet the main Stillaguamish channel near Arlington, while the Pilchuck River turns southward to be emptied into the Snohomish River near the town of Snohomish. Finally, both the Stillaguamish River and the Snohomish River empty into the Puget Sound: the Stillaguamish into Port Susan and the Snohomish into Possession Sound, only about 12 nautical miles apart.

About 13,000 years ago a massive eruption exploded Glacier Peak shaping the mountain's western flanks and forming the Stillaguamish River headwaters near the town of Darrington, where just a few feet separate it from the Skagit River basin.

Planning to paddle these interesting waterway diversions, I entered into the Stillaguamish at Hat slough just off Boe Road south of Florence on a chilled, wet, and misty October morning. My intention was to explore the mudflat areas of Port Susan and venture into the Skagit mudflats via the South Pass and the West Pass of the north Stillaguamish river channel and then kayak south to finish my paddle at Kayak Point. It is during this time of year when scores of migratory birds are filling up the delta to spend the winter and early spring here or just use it as a temporary stopover for refueling before continuing on to their final winter destinations further south.

I needed at least four to five feet of tidal change in this waterway in order to travel comfortably, and today conditions were even better. There was a break in the rain, it was partially cloudy and the filtered sunlight penetrated the mist giving me some visibility. It had been raining hard for the past few days with strong gusty winds. The river was visibly high and somewhat murky. Gobs of logs, branches, and leaves were floating with the current, making my progress quite ambitious. Paddling through the crisp air engulfed by serenity I could see golden and amber fallen leaves sticking to my blades each time they were lifted above the water line.

Until the early 1900s, the Stillaguamish, or the Stilly, as it is fondly called by the locals, had been flowing directly into the lower portion of Skagit Bay at Stanwood. Then the main channel was diverted southward by local authorities into Hat Slough, and from there into Port Susan, to prevent flooding within the Stanwood township and to free additional farmland. Today the old channel is left as a narrow secondary connection into south Skagit Bay via West Pass. It also connects to Port Susan via the South Pass outlet. These two passes, together with Davis Slough, link Skagit Bay and Port Susan during high tides.

The two deltas of the Skagit and Stillaguamish encompass an enormous estuarine maze where sloughs, channels, and streams are interconnected to form highly diverse flora and fauna; it is a dream exploration arena for paddlers.

As I was reflecting on the history of the Stilly and the river's amazing estuarial complexities, I was entering the Hat Slough mouth into the open shallow delta by the broad river opening where willows, tall and small, dominate the banks of its many narrow side channels. By now, the clouds started vanishing, displaying blue skies with excellent visibility. I could see as far to the west as the snow-capped Olympic range and as far to the north and the east as the Cascade range with Mount Baker's looming white snow blanket.

Viewing Mount Baker from the kayak cockpit is always spectacular. I can't get tired of it, and many a time I feel that seeing it is the only reason to be out there kayaking.

The Stillaguamish River runs through Hat Slough and opens up widely into the Puget Sound forming there an enormous maze of sloughs, channels, and streams of diverse flora and fauna.

Hat Slough is vast and elaborate with a magnificent 360 degrees vista where one can explore the estuary for hours, in absolutely total solitude observing the birds, seals, river otters, and occasionally gray whales that forage at the entrance. The slough was quite shallow and in places I had to shove the kayak with my hands against the river bottom in order to move to a deeper course. Huge stems, with elaborate dry roots turned upward, covered the shallows as if intending to dam the entrance and control the water flow into the slough.

Hundreds of shorebirds, ducks, and sea gulls, were active in the shallows and the exposed mudflats. I could also see three bald eagles, perched on tree trunks scouting the flats and two more wading in the shallows with their heads down. As I was paddling the sound of the rippling waves coming in one after the other filled the air as the flood began to build up. Before long, it felt as if I were at the mercy of one giant ocean machine noisily churning and mixing the slough water with the bay water in one gigantic wheel of motion. I kept paddling vigorously, fearing that if I paused for even one second, I would be pushed backward into the flow.

Moving into the deeper waters of Port Susan I headed north toward South Pass. A group of curious seals followed me for

The Stillaguamish delta is a dream exploration arena for kayakers and other floaters.

a while, at about 25 yards away from my starboard, giving me a clue about the water depth as I was approaching the pass. The pass channel was narrow but visible. I entered the mouth easily even though just outside the course it was still muddy. Scores of shorebirds, mostly dunlins and pectoral sandpipers, were busy feeding at the south bank shallows, all in concert with each other. The dunlins took off in a buzz as soon as I got to about a kayak length from the exposed muddy shores. The sandpipers didn't mind my presence.

Shortly I forked into West Pass and glanced at the busy bridge connecting Stanwood with Camano Island. In fact, this narrow channel is what separates Camano from the mainland to make it an island. Skagit Bay greeted me with a huge flock of mixed surf and white-winged scoters, floating just outside the mouth of the pass where the incoming tide was now inundating the remaining exposed flats. As soon as these large ducks noticed me they took off with a loud explosion, beating with their webbed feet on the water film, gliding for a second or two inches above the water and then landed, heads up, with a conspicuous bustling splash 100 yards away. It was now time to turn back and head to Port Susan; Kayak Point was six miles away.

The setting evening sun illuminating in reddish-pink hues the distant Cascade peaks was now leading my way south. The calm bay and its shoreline features have changed markedly since I entered the waters a few hours earlier. The grassy flats were now gone, and the obvious delineation of the entrances to the sloughs was no longer conspicuous as seen at low tide. Water was everywhere, now at high tide.

This new scene exemplified the incredible estuarine stratification changes caused by the periodic gravitational circulation. The tide-generated turbulence together with surface winds stir and mix diverse layers of residual organic matter both vertically and horizontally. The mixing and stirring is fundamentally vital for primary (plant) production. Myriad species of plants and animals depend on this cyclic change.

It is an energy-driven process cutting across various trophic levels where the use and dependency of each species involved, are determined by natural selection along evolutionary timescales. This twice-a-day tidal cycle determines the habitats for intra and inter-specific competition, selecting organisms which can be maintained and become prolific in this environment.

As I continued my paddling south,

scores of diving ducks were foraging closer to the newly formed shoreline. I headed there trying to get a closer look at the rapidly changing scenes and as I did, I just passed four bald eagles, perched on high stems looming out of the shallows like sentinels, ready to strike a fish. A moment later I saw, to my delight, a rough-legged hawk soaring low above the exposed marsh and farm fields searching for rodents and songbirds with two northern harriers also circling low. In the distance I could also see a lone American kestrel perched on a snag, while a couple of red-tailed hawks were soaring high above the land.

Being able to observe such a variety and number of raptor species in search for similar food tells me that competition for food here is low and that this natural habitat is in good health and that it is productive.

In nature, when food is abundant, rivalry between individuals dependent on the same resources is not apparent. But when resources are limited, sheer competition is obvious, setting in motion the forces of natural selection. Competitors tend to detect the precise timing to yield to the stronger, more deterministic predator, since energy is a precious commodity and battling for a loss is neither in question nor feasible. The tidal fluctuations in the Stilly and Skagit deltas often witness periodical physical and biological perturbations which may temporarily change the habitats' natural constituencies. These open communities,

50

The setting sun illuminating in reddish-pink hues the distant Cascade range.

where plants and animals assemble by random opportunities, dispersal abilities and time, are highly resilient and when species wealth is reduced, they eventually bounce back by means of their historical resilient capabilities.

As I moved closer to Kayak Point for my take-out, I saw the tidal flat sections of Port Susan replaced by urban settings touching the shoreline. Backyard lawns tacked within manicured gardens dominated the landscape. As I saw the human encroachment deep into the wilderness sections of the tidal flats, surrounded by air pollution, land barriers and toxic floats from cars on paved roads and from synthetic chemicals from local farms, I wondered how much longer this resiliency will last.

52

Shorebirds fly over the Snohomish River estuary.

4

Snohomish River and Sloughs

Sunset at the mouth of the Snohomish River

It was early in the morning, a combination of mist and fog, when I parked my car about 30 yards from the north bank of the Sultan River, just under the Washington Highway 2 bridge west of the town of Sultan. This convenient put-in site by the Sultan River is a gateway to the Skykomish River which, at about 50 yards away, runs briskly westward. Due to the length of the Snohomish course, I had decided to navigate it in two parts on two separate days: the upper river, starting at the confluence of the Sultan with the Skykomish downriver to the Snohomish and further down to the town of Snohomish; and the lower river with the vast delta from the town of Snohomish to Langus Park across from Everett.

Although it was wet, I anticipated the weather to clear up later on in the morning. On this early October day, the deciduous vegetation was in its peak color change, and the mist added an unsurpassed beauty to the occasion. The headwaters of the Skykomish River—a tributary of the Snohomish River—are in the higher Cascades, in the Steven Pass area, between Mount Hinman

The headwaters of the Skykomish River, a tributary of the Snohomish River, are in the rugged Cascades region of Steven Pass.

54

in the south and the Skykomish Peak—Caddy Pass in the north. The Skykomish has an impressive watershed with fast dashing tributaries like the North Fork Skykomish River, the South Fork Skykomish River, the Beckler River, Foss River, and Miller River to name a few.

The Sultan River originates at Del Campo Peak and the Crested Buttes range and moves an enormous amount of clear waters from both Spada Lake and Lake Chaplain into the Skykomish River. The Sultan is shallow and swift at its confluence

with the Skykomish where there are ample sandy beaches. This morning, masses of spawning pink salmon were literally covering the waters along the shoreline with numerous others moving upriver where they were met by a flock of hungry gulls, one bald eagle, and two fishermen.

I squeezed myself quietly into the cockpit and pushed onto the rushing waters of the confluence. The Skykomish River meanders along colorful vegetated banks and flat sand bars. I could see groups of pink salmon with their humpback form swim within the deeper sections of the sand bars dodging the kayak. Pink salmon spend only two years in the ocean before maturing to return to the rivers for spawning. There are two genetically distinct populations of pink salmon (fondly known as "pinkies"): even-year and odd-year spawning pinkies.

The Snohomish River and its western tributaries, being major spawning grounds within the Puget Sound system, maintain the two populations with their respective schedules. The Skykomish River hosts the odd-year pinkies only. Baker Bay situated at the mouth of the Columbia River marks the southern geographical limit of these two pink salmon populations. In late September, mature fat individuals start their energy-demanding journey up river, to deposit eggs in clean coarse gravel beds in shady areas within shallow pools where the current is fast. A few months later, during the early spring, the quick growing newborns move closer to the river estuary to gain additional weight before entering the open ocean. As of 2007, pink salmon in the Puget Sound waterways, like the other

Remains of pink salmon coming to spawn in the clear gravelly shallow pools near the confluence of the Sultan and Skykomish Rivers are consumed by an array of predators during early fall.

The Skykomish River meanders along pristine areas of steep forested terrain and dense colorful banks skirting numerous sand bars along its course to the Snohomish River.

56

salmonids, are on the decline. The reason: habitat changes along the rivers and estuaries and rising toxicity levels in the Puget Sound—all caused by intense human land use in a rapidly growing economy.

Nine miles of down-river kayaking brought me to the town of Monroe where the river meanders along farming fields and urban settings before it meets with the Snoqualmie River. I was now swiftly approaching the confluence of the Skykomish and the Snoqualmie. Right in front of me there were two islands which occupied almost the whole width of the river.

I moored on a sunny open sandy gravel beach located on a narrow strip between these two islands just east of the Snoqualmie channel which runs along a densely vegetated elongated spit. I stripped out of my life-vest and the skirt, grabbed a sweet energy bar, and ventured out onto the sand bars to explore this area where the two rivers merge. The waters were swift in spite of the shallows.

A few pink salmon carcasses lay at the edge of the sand bars, where an assembly of five glaucous-winged gulls, two mew gulls, and two bald eagles were busy scavenging. There was no apparent rivalry between the

Monroe Valley along the Skykomish River path is a productive farming community

birds as food was plentiful. At the edge of a sand bar, yards from the confluence, I saw two great blue herons—one in a cattail lagoon, and one in the open current—gracefully standing still anticipating a strike. These birds were so focused on their foraging that they ignored me altogether. Perhaps the noise made by the rushing waters helped in buffering the sound of my approach. I sat on top of a large dry log and watched the eagles, the gulls, and the herons. Not more than 30 yards of shallow waters separated the four species.

On other occasions with such a collection of birds, I had witnessed eagles' intense predatory drive toward gulls or herons, but not today. The only interest these eagles showed was in the dying fish. Likewise, no apparent fear was shown by the gulls or the herons. Ecological dynamics of getting the most bang for the buck was in its essence; the eagles were optimizing their valuable time and efforts on the easily accessible and more profitable food: fish.

Back into the kayak I slowly maneuvered into the confluence of the two rivers actually entering the Snohomish River. The Skykomish and Snoqualmie rivers empty two huge watersheds when they merge together to form the Snohomish River. The waters flow with roaring intensity and as I was gliding into the swift current of the Snohomish I felt a wave of ecstasy and elation. It felt as if these two mighty rivers were offering me on top of my kayak to the Snohomish to take me all the way to the Puget Sound.

The current was very powerful with all that water rushing into the narrow channel. Some riffles and then a class two rapid greeted me as I approached the bridge of Hwy 522. I skirted the right bank, where the path looked calmer, increased my paddling strokes, and swiftly passed under the bridge into a deep green quieter flow for another two miles. The river now formed an S shape turn with nestled small islands and sand bars. The densely vegetated banks were replaced with farmlands.

Pied-billed grebes, buffleheads, mergansers, mallards, and geese were swimming and flying in front of the kayak keeping me company as I was dodging between these small islands and the shallows. For the next four miles, all the way to the town of Snohomish, the river channel narrowed and became challenging to navigate through the intricate system of the surrounding wetlands, sloughs, and dammed farmlands.

A group of about twenty American wigeon ducks swarmed in the small cove at the Pilchuck River confluence. These ducks whistled loudly and then dashed a few yards further upriver, causing a growling heron to take off as I passed by them. Clouds were coming in fast from the Sound, and the sun started diminishing. In less than a quarter

mile I pulled into Cady Park to end this stretch of the river.

From the town of Snohomish, the Snohomish River meanders westward through wetlands, farmlands and urban settings. This area contains one of the fastest urban developments along the Interstate 5 corridor. As the river approaches Everett it turns into a huge estuary system of sloughs that intertwine around islands, bogs, and marshes forming a large delta on both sides of I-5. The delta at the river's mouth is mostly an industrial port, while the east side of I-5 is partly preserved as wetlands and partly used as farmland.

Late in June, on a clear sunny morning I entered the Snohomish River at Cady Park boat launch. My plan was to paddle the Snohomish River and the estuary, all the way to the river's mouth mud flats at Possession Sound north of the city of Everett, a total of 18 miles. I had chosen a day when the tidal differences are insignificant, so that I could take my time to explore the estuary and the flats without having to worry about getting stuck in the mud at low waters.

The river was high and fast and I was traveling at around seven knots, enjoying the soft breeze caressing my face. Shortly before the Hwy 9 bridge, out of nowhere, two power boats came rushing from behind, passing my kayak at the port forming unnecessarily large wakes that bumped

The Skykomish River near the confluence with the Snoqualmie River.

against my bow and sides flushing my skirt with water. The noise made by the passing cars on the bridge must have prevented me from hearing the approaching boats and be prepared for their rush. This incident immediately reminded me that I was kayaking in a busy urban setting although the banks were still densely vegetated and surrounded by open fields.

Two miles later I turned north onto Ebey Slough which hugs the wetland area to the east of the estuary system along South Ebey Island. This sluggish and peaceful channel snakes mostly through cultivated land and some marshes: all relics from earlier wetlands which were extensively diked during the beginning of the twentieth century to be replaced by farmlands.

Two common mergansers and a belted kingfisher took off as they detected my kayak completing a curve in the channel. Surprisingly, a lone great blue heron in a grassy nook by the shoreline didn't budge when I glided by. The banks of the channel are sparsely vegetated here which enabled me to also look for upland wildlife.

Seven miles into Ebey Slough I entered Steamboat Slough which bisects Spencer and Ebey islands. Two adult ospreys, perching on a tall skinny snag scouted my

Feeding time at the osprey nest. The mud flats, when inundated at high tides, are a busy channel for commercial and pleasure boats coming and going to Port Gardner, Everett.

60

approach into a narrow side channel which connects to Union Slough. This tiny pass of less than 70 yards cuts Spencer Island through an expansive marsh forming North Spencer Island. This section of the estuary is known as The Big Hole. It is densely covered with tall grass, cattail, and low shrubs filled with fresh water and supports diverse avian life.

As I was kayaking through this water system I encountered the largest number of bird species: grebes, cormorants, several species of ducks and herons, several raptor species, song birds and several mammals like beaver, river otter, coyote, raccoon, and muskrat. This environment is as diverse as a walk-in museum of natural history, and one can find here all the species listed in a field guide to northwestern fauna. No doubt the Snohomish delta is immense. With the complex estuarine habitats connecting with the Stilly and Skagit deltas, only 12 and 15 miles to the north, through sloughs, streams and marshes, these deltas are of a scale unsurpassed in northwestern Washington.

Natural habitats are complex entities including overwhelming detail. Physical and biological boundaries change incessantly and perpetually within continuous landscapes, governed by the laws of natural selection. Organisms move within the habitat continuum in space and time by their dispersal abilities. The niche space of each species—food, reproduction, and shelter—has to be satisfied within the continuum scale. Individuals of a species simply leave a patch within the habitat when they can no longer optimize their foraging dynamics. Individuals will leave if food items are hard to find because they are absent or because of keen competition with others. Or they will leave if reproduction is hampered because of lack of shelter, or because of obsessive predators. River otters, for example, move constantly from place to place within their local range according to the depletion or increase of their food availability. An osprey will cut on its hunting bouts if not successful and immediately move into more profitable patches. Double-crested cormorants, common mergansers or grebes will leave a lake or a lagoon if a few dives will not produce a catch.

Advanced human development is an ongoing reality. A flock of American wigeon ducks tries to make its best within Possession Sound and Jetty Island waters.

Patches of species richness and their abundance is indicative of a preferred location supporting calm resting, safe shelter, or a rich foraging arena. The Snohomish River Estuary represents this kind of natural habitat. This preserve, set aside by the county from a larger natural setting, is now surrounded by industrial urban sprawl and farmlands and crisscrossed by congested automobile corridors including Interstate 5 and Hwy 2, and is now for all practical purposes an island of ecological entities.

However, it is still part of the Snohomish-Stilly-Skagit estuary continuum. In order to maintain the ecological viability of this entire continuum, it is urgently important to preserve and manage these waterways, keeping them undisturbed and free of toxic substances.

I continued my paddle along the Union Slough waterway's narrow channel meandering along Smith and North Spencer Islands. On top of several pilings, a number of osprey nests could be easily seen, with

Union Slough. In an effort to preserve and add natural habitats to the greater Snohomish River estuary and delta which lost more than eighty percent of its natural tidal marshes and mudflats to human development during the early 1900, about twenty four acres of tidal estuary was recovered by the community of Everett a few years ago, resulting in a vibrant slough.

62

several birds nesting, and others hovering about. With the long sunset, the orange-red colored clouds in the horizon kept changing their form and shape at each curve of the slough. Even the noisy highway overpasses, the huge mill yard towers, the numerous pilings and docks along the waterline appeared as grand silhouettes against the bright reddish-yellow-orange rays of the settling evening.

The passing gulls, herons and ospreys added their share to the surrounding beauty. The confluence of Union and Steamboat sloughs, which is also the opening to Possession Sound, was busy with fishing boats retreating to Port Gardner for the night. More ospreys could be seen returning to their nests on top of the wood pilings spread within the mud flats.

The tide was high at the moment enabling me to paddle close to the Smith Island shoreline to have a closer look at those enormous nests. A series of huge log booms blocked my route as I tried to get near the tall grass cover at the shallow shoreline. The floating logs barred to the shallows like an island occluded my way to the northwest tip of Jetty Island.

The evening breeze which was soft and calm a while ago started to gain force, creating surging waves. With the tight booms, there was no open alley to let me pass through to get to Jetty Island. The only thing to do was to detour the booms from

Seen from Possession Sound and Jetty Island, Everett's industrial pollutants contribute daily tons of toxins to the surrounding natural environment of Puget Sound.

the north and paddle toward deeper waters of the sound nearing Priest Point at the mainland and then cross against the waves toward Jetty Island. Jetty Island is a two-mile-long artificial island created as a jetty to protect Port Gardner, Everett's sea port, from the open waters of Possession Sound.

As I was moving along the shallow west shore the wind subsided, the waves disappeared and the twilight skies altered colors by the moment. A group of five California sea lions was lying calmly on a sandy beach completely ignoring me. Sea gulls and a small group of wigeon ducks were active in the shallows and on the beach further south where the island narrows dramatically

retaining only a narrow band of rocks as breakers.

As the red sun touched the horizon I entered the port waters and then the mouth of the Snohomish River at Preston Point, glided between Everett and Ferry Baker Island where cormorants and herons crossed my path on the way to their night colony roost. The glistening light illuminating the city of Everett and its industrial legs gave me a feeling of elation and jubilation, so intense was the beauty of the setup. Finally, 12 hours since my put-in, I landed at Langus Riverfront Park and took my last photo of the darkening daylight

Mama wood duck is followed by her ducklings on the Sammamish River.

5

Sammamish River to Shilshole Bay

The Sammamish River meanders along Redmond's Marymoor Park, where the banks are heavily vegetated and preserved, supporting diverse wildlife.

I pulled my kayak tacked to the cart for one quarter of a mile along the paved trails of Idylwood Park heading to a sandy beach on the southwest corner of Lake Sammamish just a mile from the Sammamish River headwaters. It was late September early in the morning. A low layer of transparent fog hovered tenderly above the water ascending slowly toward the river's inception. The air was filled with the scent of a fall dawn.

A few gulls and mallards were resting on an elongated shoal not far away and more mallards floated towards me almost touching the kayak as I was readying for a push into the calm cold water. Slowly, awakening my shoulder muscles, I brushed the west shoreline of the lake skirting the small boat docks planted within the tall grass in front of a row of luxury condos erected along the banks right on the waterline.

My plan for the day was to explore the Sammamish River waterway all the way to its terminus where it empties into Lake Washington, about ten miles away, and then for another 13 miles to cross Lake Washington to the channel which connects to Lake Union and then on to Shilshole Bay in the Puget Sound.

Lake Sammamish collects its waters from some unimpressive tributaries. The lake's watershed is small and is locked tightly between the much larger Snohomish River and Green River watersheds. The uniqueness of the Sammamish watershed is that it connects two major freshwater lakes, Lake Sammamish and Lake Washington, to the Puget Sound. These lakes supply drinking and irrigation water to a meta-urban habitation. The Sammamish River empties its waters to Lake Washington from the north, while the Cedar River waters empty into Lake Washington from the south.

As I entered the Sammamish River, I noticed the pristine and natural surroundings. I was meandering with the narrow river along Redmond's Marymoor Park where the banks were heavily vegetated and preserved; so much so, that in some places

The Sammamish River watershed is locked tightly between the much larger Snohomish and Green river watersheds. The Sammamish watershed connects two major freshwater lakes, Lake Sammamish and Lake Washington, which supply drinking and irrigation water to a meta-urban habitation, and links them to the Puget Sound.

where trees, shrubs and tall grass abound, my 17 feet long kayak could barely fit the course. Four ring-necked duck males dashed into the water from a sheltered grassy spot on the south bank as I dodged by, anxiously disappearing ahead of my eyes at the channel's turn.

Shortly thereafter, I noticed a colorful green heron moving slightly from its numb inanimate pose in a shady spot when it detected me. The solitary green herons are very secretive and patient when on the hunt. They blend perfectly with the dense vegetation of slow moving waters or marshes. These wading birds have learned to use tools for fishing through evolutionary adaptation. They drop a feather, a leaf, a stick or a berry, or even an insect, on the water as bait and wait for a fish to surface, or a small frog to jump forward before they strike. They can be found in Washington year round but some spend the winters in western Mexico.

Leaving Marymoor Park, I was now flowing with the river under busy traffic bridges, along industrial parks, and close to homes. The city of Redmond is one of a series of wall-to-wall contemporary suburbs explosively developed during the early 1990s. Here the roads are wide and the houses blend with extensive vegetative growth. When I drive the streets I feel I'm passing through a park. But from the kayak, the constant hum of the active streets and highways was buzzing in my ears. Still, staring at the river course and its diverse

vegetation along the banks I decided to ignore it. The water flow was moderate and I was making good progress.

Five miles later, the river cut through a set of county parks and marshes. A consortium of towns along the river banks turned a stretch of three plus miles of open space into parks and a lengthy trail—the Sammamish River Trail—for hikers, joggers, skaters, and bikers. The trail, a converted railroad right-of-way, 11 miles in length, is part of the "locks to Lakes Corridor". The incredible views of the Sammamish River Valley and its Cascade foothills, and Mount Rainier also motivate non-motorized commuters to use the trail extensively as a link between suburban cities and Seattle.

I parked my kayak at a small eddy located at the north bank just yards past a pedestrian bridge at Sixty Acres Park to stretch my legs and eat an apple. The River Trail was inundated with joggers, bikers and walkers, although it was only a little after 8 AM. The air was clear and cool. The sun just initiated its morning warmth. I let myself into the trail and joined the exercising crowd and commuters for a short walk enjoying the sound of the flowing river from the land. I was pleasantly surprised to see how intensely the trail is being used by people.

Back into the kayak I paddled through the open space parkland and then passed a section of farmland on my starboard and an industrial setting on my port. The banks

67

Floating through the Sammamish River preserved parkland.

68

were all densely vegetated and the marginal setbacks to the developed area became more extensive, allowing a better blend with the natural upland ecological systems. The air got somewhat warmer, and a soft wind tendered my upper torso. The river was clean with a few drifting small logs, branches, and leaves near the shorelines.

These were splendid moments, when everything seemed to fit perfectly into place. Every now and then I felt compelled to exchange greetings with the people who use the river trail which stretches alongside the north bank. Even though I was the only one on the river, I was certainly not alone.

Nearly two decades ago, social ecologist Dr. Jim Kent and I introduced the notion of Bio-Social Ecosystems, a concept which is based on the tenet that people and nature, in a human-geographic unit, can co-exist in productive harmony and ensure the continuity of natural and social resources for future generations. We defined "productive harmony" as a healthy, balanced state of an environment where both its social and natural diverse resources have high levels of permanence.

Social resources are the people found in a self-defined geographic area: their survival networks and their self-subscribed boundaries around various living patterns and activities. Diversity, in this context, refers to the range of options people have open in a human geographic unit for cultural and economic activities: whom to associate with (networks), where to live (settlement), how to earn a living (work), how to get and give help (support services), and where and how to have fun (recreation).

Natural resources are all the physical and biological attributes of a given geographic area, except the people. Such resources are renewable (timber, wildlife, water, solar energy) and non-renewable (minerals, fossil fuels). Diversity in this context is the variety and availability of natural resources which are interdependent in a systematic

The monstrous cement pillars of Interstate 405 and Washington hwy 522 are noisy reminders of the causes for water and biota deterioration of the Sammamish River as it flows to Lake Washington.

Mount Rainier at 14,411 feet high looms above Seattle's Lake Washington.

70

way such that each affects the viability of all other components. Permanence refers to the perceptions people have that the resources of their human-geographic unit will be around for some time to come. For social resources, permanence includes people's sense of stability coupled with their ability to participate in, predict, and control events affecting their future. Where natural resources are concerned, permanence means that the yield of both renewable and non-renewable resources will continue well into the future.

As I was floating through this parkland, I could appreciate the scenery here as an expression of the bio-social ecosystems concept. I could clearly recognize here the relationship between the physical and social environments forming a cultural alignment of the informal community system (people) with the formal institutional systems (government) which may link us to a tangible permanence.

But a thought enters my mind—can this local concept of a balanced bio-social ecosystem be applied on a larger scale as well? As I am contemplating the larger picture, I find it dreadfully sad to realize that most of humankind is not yet ready to accept the concept of bio-social ecosystems.

Government and administrators are too busy overexploiting energy sources and securing corporate self-interest and power while spending less time working together with neighborhoods and their communities on fundamental environmental and social issues. Perhaps, with today's spurred degradation of the environment, permanence as described above is an illusion. Maybe permanence is beyond reach.

The freeway complex of Interstate 405 and Highway 522 disrupted my contemplation as I passed under the extensive structures and close to their enormous rounded pillars. Luckily the noise faded out as I entered a set of ninety degree curves with private homes of various sizes along both banks.

Groups of mallards and mergansers accompanied my kayak to the sandy beach at the Kenmore Park boat launch. This site is about a quarter mile from the entrance to Lake Washington. At 10 AM I was four to five hours from Shilshole Bay. The weather was perfectly warm with negligible wind, and it was still early in the day. I had ample time for this stretch.

When I entered Lake Washington after the short rest, rounding a small island located at the mouth, the area was shallow

Union Bay, Lake Washington, is the entrance to the greater Seattle metro area waterway. Small green islands, with side channels to explore marshes and lagoons abound. One can easily see the enormous value of this place by counting the numerous kayaks, sit-on-tops, and canoes that roam within the swampy channels.

Portage Bay is the arm that links Lake Washington with Lake Union. The loud hum from the I-5 bridges can not be ignored. The waterway shores are lined with exotic houseboats, numerous restaurants, shipyards and docks.

72

on all sides of the island, and I could barely paddle. I moved over to the lake's east bank just in time before three motor boats entered the river at moderate speed using the deep narrow channel by the river's north bank, loading the river entrance with a growling wake. Large concentrations of coots, scaup, canvasbacks, and buffleheads, combined with gulls, and double-crested cormorants, occupied the southeast side of the lake opening, feeding in the shallows completely ignoring the boats roaming in the vicinity

and the constant noise made by the landing and departing sea-planes.

Private homes with big lawns extending to the water line and boats tied to long docks carpeted the shoreline all the way to Champaign Point where I crossed the lake to Sand Point on the west side. The ride was smooth and pleasant. The air was so clear and crisp that I could see in great detail Mount Rainier's enormous snow caps and glaciers to the south.

After about eight miles of paddling I

The Small Lock at Salmon Bay is the channel for kayakers to descend fifteen feet from the bay's fresh waters to the salt waters of Shilshole Bay and Puget Sound.

pulled into a small grassy cove with a narrow stretch of sandy beach which I spotted at the northwest corner of Union Bay. Union Bay is the entrance to the greater Seattle area waterway and its northern shoreline is part of the University of Washington campus. The area is beautiful with small green islands and side channels to explore marshes and lagoons. Although it is an urban setting—with highways and bridges cutting through the south section of these small islands, with large and small power boats leaving and entering the waterways— the diverse plant configuration, the tall trees and the general topography of the area give it a feeling of a remote rainforest. One can easily see the enormous recreational value of this place simply by counting the numerous kayaks, sit-on-tops, and canoes that roam within the narrow swampy channels.

Gliding through Montlake Cut and under Montlake Bridge I entered Lake Union via Portage Bay. Now the loud hum from I-5 was beyond my ability to ignore. The constant sound escorted me along the exotic houseboats, numerous restaurants, shipyards and docks, the skyscrapers of downtown Seattle, and the Needle, to a flat tiny beach on the west corner of Gas Works Park where I rested momentarily and examined in detail the pretty urban course I have just traced paddling in an industrial municipal setting.

It was 2 PM when I resumed my cross to Puget Sound. Getting there I had to paddle through the Locks and then descend 15 feet from the fresh waters to the salt waters of Shilshole Bay. Kayaking on the south side I entered Lake Washington Ship Canal passing under the George Washington Bridge and the Fremont Bridge, mostly dodging the soft wakes of passing motor boats in this very busy place. I was not the only kayaker going westward. Gliding under Ballard Bridge I entered Salmon Bay and its Fisherman Terminal.

Next to the passing barges and large fishing boats, my kayak seemed like a toy as I was slowly and steadfastly following other kayakers on the path to the small lock on the south side of the channel. I grabbed and held onto a cleat mounted on the lock's wall and waited as water started to drain out and slowly level with seawater. Then, with the opening of the gates, the soft flow rushed me out into a calm Puget Sound. I have just completed the "Lakes to Locks Corridor" waterway.

6

Green River to Elliot Bay

The Green River near Fort Dent Park meanders under the busy Interstate 405. The dense vegetation with multi layered growth is preserved where development setbacks are taken into account.

It was the second week of May. I was meandering along Green Valley Road snaking off the north banks of the Green River towards Flaming Geyser State Park, my put-in spot. It was a cold dawn, and water vapors hung over the river channel. The skies were clear after a two-day rain, and the clouds have vanished during the night hours. Half an hour into sunrise I settled in my cockpit and pushed myself into a small deep pool and then ferry-angled into the fast current. The water was clear and in places shallow with small ripples. I kept the kayak in the deeper sections of the course to avoid exposed rocks and shallows. The ride was clean and fast.

In about two miles I entered a set of small rapids where the river bent a couple of times. The rapids covered the whole width of the river and at the end of an elongated island further down gained momentum to form a crescendo of waves for a stretch of fifty yards. The water level was high enough, making the kayak surf swiftly over the white waters before the river straightened onto a deeper smooth quiet channel. What a great way to start a long paddle! My destination was Fort Dent Park about 33 miles away.

The Green River collects its water from the western slopes of the Cascades south of Interstate 90 within the region of Blowout Mountain, Stampede Pass, the south flanks of Goat Mountain, and Kelly Butte. Historically, the Green River watershed was much more impressive than it is today. Two big rivers—the Cedar River to the north, and the White River to the south— emptied their waters into the Green River on its course westward, together forming a massive watershed.

Between 1900 and 1916, however, several water diversions around Lake Washington took place which altered the watershed in a major way: the Cedar, which had been flowing into the Black River draining the southern end of Lake Washington into the Green, was diverted into Lake Washington. At the completion of the construction of Washington Ship Canal's Montlake Cut linking Lake Washington with Lake Union, the water level in Lake Washington dropped almost nine feet. This situation drained the Black River out of its waters, freeing land for the

building of Renton and its surrounds.

Therefore today, the Cedar River, which collects its waters from the north flanks of Goat Mountain, Abiel Peak-Yakima Pass, and the slopes of Meadow Mountain, empties its flow into Lake Washington's south end and its watershed is part of the Seattle water system.

The White River, which originates in the north and northeast glaciers of Mount Rainier and the Dalles Ridge-Coral Pass regions, was also diverted from the Green after 1900. As a result of constant flooding within the Green and the White confluence area causing home and farm destructions in this fast growing urban area, the White River was diverted south into the Puyallup River.

All of these diversions separated White River and Cedar River from the Green and thus reduced its watershed size. The Green River runs its course via the Duwamish Waterway into Elliot Bay in the Puget Sound.

As I continued downstream the watercourse ran alongside dense woody and grassy vegetation on the river banks and numerous islands and exposed sand bars in its midst. The ride on the fast current with small size ripples every now and then was quite pleasant.

In terms of open space, this section of the river cuts through a large core of highly varied and undisturbed topography with elaborate vegetation creating a habitat

76

Today, the Green River collects its waters from the western slopes of the Cascades within Mount Baker-Snoqualmie National Forest south of I-90. Historically, the Green River watershed was much larger, encompassing the White and Cedar rivers watersheds. But during the early 1900s both the Cedar and the White rivers were cut off from the Green to solve flooding issues in the growing Auburn region.

continuity from Mount Rainier all the way down to the river's banks. The few farms and private houses dispersed widely here blend almost naturally within the woven matrix of the foliage height diversity of the region. This rural setting mixed with numerous nature preserves and state parks, keeps the banks of the Green undisturbed with ample setback zones.

As I was kayaking along this setting, I wondered how much longer this open space configuration along the river would last before it became developed. Knowing that future development is inevitable in a natural setting like this rural region, my thoughts are that dispersal planning, rather than cluster planning would be highly desirable. Scattered buildings with wide margins

The Green River during a flood.

78

leave roomy open space, keeping a vertical and horizontal continuum of the natural ecology intact with its core habitats.

A dispersal design, which intermingles widely with public lands, fits very well with island biogeography theory: flora and fauna dispersal abilities and niche availabilities remain open through a matrix of corridors. On the other hand, cluster planning, in general, tends to aggregate people and services and before you know it, the whole open space is swallowed and gone to accommodate more people and more services. My hope is that this region east of Auburn remains as we see it today.

After about sixteen miles, as the channel entered the I-5 corridor, the river changed its character. The banks were almost bare of plants and there were minimal setbacks to the developed land alongside the river. The river and the few parks along its banks are the only biotic continuum along this segment. Multilane highways and extensive noise from passing cars dominated the prosperous urban settings of Auburn, Kent, and Renton.

After nearly nine hours on the river I reached the last bend north of I-405 and landed at a tiny level spot on the south side of Fort Dent Park where Eva and Buddy greeted me warmly. I have completed the first segment of the river.

The next morning, with the first rays of the sun, I started my second segment of the Green River: the Duwamish Waterway from Fort Dent Park to Elliot Bay. In less than a mile I arrived at the confluence area of the Green River and the Black River and entered the Black River channel.

Paddling in murky waters I explored the remnants of the river that once was the outlet of Lake Washington and a significant tributary of the Green. The channel was narrow, muddy, and with no apparent flow. In about half a mile, after passing under a bottleneck of crowded highways, streets, and a quarry entrance, the river passage was blocked by King County's flood-control monstrous facility standing there like a dam.

I anchored along the north bank where I located an opening in the dense willow-berry cover and stepped out for an on-foot detour entering into a small slough, a ninety-plus acre preserve named Black River Riparian Forest, engulfed tightly by parkways on all sides. This marshy open space crisscrossed by small channels is like an island in the midst of an urban area.

Dominated by a cottonwood and alder canopy, this "island" is home to a large great blue heron nesting colony—in spite of the constant traffic noise, a bicycle path, and the forceful human development

A lone great blue heron forages at the Black River Riparian Forest preserve off the banks of the Green River near Fort Dent.

and intense activities near its banks. The survival and success of the heron nesting colony here is thanks to the Herons Forever members who since 1989 advocate for the protection and preservation of this riparian island and its surrounding ecology. More than 120 active nests were observed here that produced close to 300 fledglings. Bald Eagles prey extensively on the herons, but the colony persists.

Walking on the trail that skirts the slough from the south the loud continuous sounds coming from the dense tall cotton-wood stands was very conspicuous. Adult herons were seen coming and going from the tree stands, but the nests couldn't be seen because of the leaf coverage. This heron nursery will be active all through July.

Other wildlife species I have seen during my short stay here included pied-billed grebes, Canada geese, mallards, American wigeons, buffleheads, hooded mergansers, various song birds, and bald eagles. A muskrat and a river otter were retreating into the brush at the west entrance to the slough as I was pulling in.

This little park is not only preserved for the sake of the heron's survival. The park is more than that. It is a remainder of a much larger ecological entity. It is an island that supports a rich assembly of organisms which is part of the watershed habitat continuum.

Currently, the park is linked to the Green and to tiny other streams, to ponds, and to other viable remnants of riparian habitats that keep the urban preserve alive. I would say that the park's wetland, most likely, acts today as an important ecological core surrounded by a cemented landscape. This is the park's essence.

Returning back to the Green River main channel I continued downstream in what is now called the Duwamish River or Waterway. The river is named after the Duwamish people who dwelled within the historical Black River area. Meandering

At low tide, the Duwamish Waterway vibrates and roars as it passes through South 112 Street.

Midway in the Duwamish Waterway.

along the thinly vegetated water course under bridges and alongside highways and busy streets I was attentive to the diverse sounds echoing form all directions. I was not surprised by the lack of wildlife.

At the South 112 Street pedestrian bridge the channel curved to the north-west where a huge boulder and a few rocks covered the north bank. The Duwamish is a tidal river and fortunately I curved this rapid from its south bank section when the water here was still high. After about two more miles I floated under South Park Bridge and shortly later I parked on a gravelly beach at Duwamish Waterway Park for a rest and a stretch.

The industrial section along the Duwamish starts here at the South Park neighborhood. The waterway is the trans-porting artery of this industrial urban network via Puget Sound to the Pacific Ocean. Through years of operation both the land and the water are highly toxic where contaminants vein into the river via storm water floods, leaking pipes, and spilled oil and gasoline from ships and boats.

Viewed from the park's shoreline the place looks to me like a dumping ground.

The Duwamish Waterway entry to Elliott Bay, where Seattle's vibrant metropolis and wildlife mix.

82

And yet, there is something vibrant. The river is actually the heart of the metropolis; it distributes and receives vital goods to and from the world. The channel, neither clear nor murky, reflects efforts to keep the place clean. The federal government's EPA has been running a Superfund program within the six mile stretch to Elliot Bay for the last seven years but still, as of 2009, contaminants are pouring into the river.

I picked up an energy bar and strolled along the narrow modified shoreline toward a long heavy dock where two large forklifts were busy on the wide deck of a sizeable barge hauling out barrels and small wooden crates. The sun was still low but it warmed me up. The air was stuffed with heavy exhaust fumes. Across the river I could look at the immense Boeing Corporation air field covered with hangars and planes. Everything in the river's vicinity was bustling and vividly alive, very much so.

I maintained my kayak along the south side of the channel, paddling in slow motion, as I was passing along active docks and slow moving vessels. Just before the First Avenue Bridge I entered a small side channel on the south side covered by dense shoreline foliage. The channel with its narrow water path had elaborate shrubs and tree configurations along its banks which had several docks along their sides. A group of adult common goldeneyes were active, to my astonishment, in a pond-like nook at the far end of the slough.

Returning to the main channel I reached Kellogg Island in about two miles. I brushed the north beaches exploring the island flora and searching for birds; one lonely gull soared low. At the north tip of the island, by the shallows, I had to wait for a passing armada of fishing boats and barges making their way eastbound. It was two hours after low tide; the shallows were still largely exposed. I tucked the kayak between two denuded land strips and enjoyed the moving fleet.

A mile later where the main Duwamish channel forks at Harbor Island into south and north arteries, I took the south course and kayaked under the tall West Seattle Bridge cruising directly into mild swells in Elliot Bay. The scenery was incredible: Seattle's downtown skyscrapers, the Needle, the sport stadiums, the numerous cranes standing tall by the port piers, the flying cormorants, gulls, ducks, and herons, a fat California sea lion dozing on a spherical buoy, a ferry bounding out to the near-by islands, were all glorified by the colors of the setting sun.

I bowed toward Seacrest Marina Park where Eva and Buddy were waiting for me to land. I was reluctant to do so; I wanted to stay in the water as long as possible. Turning the kayak to all directions to get the last views of the surroundings I finally angled it spearing into the sandy beach near the park's boat launch and called it a day.

84

The Nisqually River watershed originates from the southern glaciers of Mount Rainier. When it reaches the lowlands it creates vast lush meadows.

7

Nisqually River and Delta

The Nisqually River meanders through numerous habitats of vegetated banks, sand bars, lagoons, marshes, and islets.

The Nisqually River originates from the southern slopes of Mount Rainier which is home to Nisqually Glacier, Van Troop Glacier, Kautz Glacier, and South Tahoma Glacier. The melting waters of these glaciers are cascading down from steep crevasses and ravines into the main Nisqually watercourse alongside Washington Highway 706.

Throughout its course, the Nisqually collects large amounts of water from steep tributaries originating in the surrounding mountains, which flow forcefully with copious amounts of water up to Alder Dam where their force is controlled. Then, the river meanders for forty-five more miles, cutting through the lowland region south of Tacoma, before it empties into the Puget Sound east to the town of Lacey where it forms an immense estuary and tidal flats.

The Nisqually River watershed courses

a rather short distance from its headwaters to the Puget Sound through numerous diverse environments and is therefore one of the more elaborate and complex watersheds found west of the Cascades. The last twelve miles of the river run in part undisturbed through the Nisqually tribal land, where they support diverse riparian habitats. This last section is superb for sea kayaking flotation.

The day after Thanksgiving I launched at McKenna Park just east of the Hwy 507 bridge. It was a clear, cool morning following seven days of incessant rain. As I was paddling, I could see some scattered exposed rocks which were easily negotiable, and the river was lively with a good water level. In about five miles, just past the turbulent junction with the merging rugged

Muck Creek on my starboard, the river entered into a narrow passage.

I started gliding through a set of meanders dominated by extensive elongated, spear-like, sand bars skirting the banks, forming in places temporary islands with lagoon-like channels. The river was swift but I arrested the firm speed of the kayak to enjoy this magic scenery. Both sides of the river are heavily vegetated and swampy. The river path is walled on both sides by steep forested bluffs, 200 to 400 feet in height, where narrow creeks and ravines enter the main stream to form swamps, oxbow ponds, and motionless channels.

I took my time here. I stopped often, examining the surroundings for birds and mammals. This was a zoologist's paradise. By now I had seen two bald eagles, one golden eagle, four great blue herons, groups of mallards, common mergansers, buffleheads, killdeers, pied-billed grebes, belted kingfishers, a soaring red-tailed hawk, and ample song bird species. Within a stretch of half a mile twice I saw river otters bask on the sand and dive for fish in the calm waters.

There was not a human soul in sight, not a human sound in the distance. All I could hear was the crystal clear notes of flowing water brushing the rocks and plants along the stream pathway and a symphony of bird calls and songs. A lively kingfisher landed on a small cottonwood tree next to me, studying the colorful water insects

86

Nisqually River, approaching the I-5 bridge.

fluttering among the plants and hovering inches above the water where a giant bull-frog peeped at them.

This sanctuary, where I come and linger to observe and listen, feels like a remote wilderness. Yet I know that I am only a few miles away from a busy urban environment. Venturing into a tiny oxbow pond I observed a green heron, perfectly camouflaged, standing on a drifting log, totally ignoring me as I was passing by, and a few yards further on a muskrat, frightened by my appearance splashed into the water from a nearby grassy mound. A tiny winter wren was following me, twittering, as I returned to the main channel where a northern harrier soared low above the banks searching for prey.

Can this place still be considered a wilderness? How does one define wilderness when our large open spaces shrink constantly?

Riparian habitats like the one I was in are complex and highly productive. Their foliage layers, vertical and horizontal, are elaborate and diverse. The riparian vegetation matrix is both temporally and spatially heterogeneous as a result of daily

A raccoon is napping on top of a tall tree by the Nisqually River estuary.

The Nisqually delta at Nisqually Reach, the southern tip of Puget Sound. A flock of dunlin is feeding erratically at the muddy flats minutes before yielding to the incoming tidal waters.

and seasonal submerging and emerging fluvial changes. These daily and seasonal fluctuations in flow and level affect plant and animal productivity. But, thanks to these variations, numerous habitat types are formed: banks, lagoons, small islands, marshes, and uplands.

Riparian plant biomass is immense and therefore can support rich fauna. In general, in a riparian ecosystem, where multiple food web layers are found, species diversity increases with increased productivity up to a point. The abundance of each species there will fluctuate with the changing scales of the habitat types due to fluvial perturbations, but the species richness will most likely stay stable.

Unfortunately, the constantly increasing human encroachments into such riparian habitats, contaminate the water or reduce water flow, wounding and bringing these productive areas to an absolute lifeless state. In the face of these shrinking habitats, any secluded life-enriched area like this could be called wilderness, even if it is not vast.

Close to noon I approached the railroad bridge and landed on a sandy spit for a stretch to check the tide predictions for the Nisqually flats. Although the middle of the main channel at the river's mouth is

The Nisqually River delta at day's end. Mount Rainier looms above the estuary as the incoming tidal waters slowly cover the grassy flats.

deep, I would need at least two feet of water covering the mud flats for negotiating the sea kayak. The predicted tidal change for the day was around 2 PM, when incoming water from the Sound was expected.

By the railroad bridge I watched two fishermen try their luck. A group of mallards and a few common mergansers were active not far away downstream taking advantage of the calm water in a large eddy. The place was quiet and peaceful in spite of the urban setting nearby.

Thirty minutes later I settled in the cockpit and entered the swift flow. The river meandered gently as it approached the bridge of Interstate 5. The noise level from the passing cars increased sharply, but faded out when I entered the Nisqually National Wildlife Refuge less than a mile downriver.

Midway in the estuary on top of a couple of cottonwood trees not more than one hundred yards apart I located two raccoons napping. They were lying there quite comfortably, legs leaning forward and heads tucked within their shoulders.

Further down I snapped a picture of two peregrine falcons perching on a branched cottonwood. At a shallow spit by the north bank of the river's mouth I sighted a few harbor seals observing my intentions.

The incoming tide was filling the shallow mud flats that expand into the bay. As I rounded the spit, I saw a group of mixed seals and California sea lions active at the entrance, probably trapping chum salmon moving into their spawning nooks upriver.

Everything was calm and beautiful when suddenly two jet boats, camouflaged to match the marsh coloration, zoomed into the flats inlets loaded with duck hunters behaving as though they owned the wildlife refuge. A large flock of dunlins feeding nervously at the grassy flats took off abruptly, forming an enormous cloud. While making an effort to land where they had taken off from, they kept their flight formation tight, making synchronized sharp turns, inches above my head, as if signaling me to move away.

The incoming water was approaching the exposed grass at the edge of the flats at an accelerated pace now. I moved to deeper waters; instantly, the birds landed as one unit resuming their erratic feeding motions seconds before the mud would yield to the water covering the dunlins' last morsels. As the water filled the flats I was increasingly able to kayak close to a large a concentration of various ducks, western grebes, and sea gulls.

The Puget Sound was calm with no wind, and only the murmur of the rolling ripples of the incoming tide was noticeable.

After spending an hour enjoying the mud flats and the beautiful snow capped Mount Rainier standing tall as if stacked directly from the river's east bank, I headed west toward the mouth of McAllister Creek for more exploration. As the sun was setting, sinking behind the horizon I landed at the Lure Beach boat launch at Nisqually Head.

Dunlins in aerobatic performance.

92

Bellingham Bay is the north gate to the greater Puget Sound. The bay is heaven to paddlers and other boats navigating the expansive waters around the San Juan Islands.

TWO

San Juan Islands

The beautiful San Juan Islands as seen at dusk. Countless sea kayak put-in sites are scattered along their shores.

94

Chuckanut Bay is Bellingham Bay's crown jewel with its coves and rocky bluffs towered with trees.

8

Lummi Island – Bellingham Bay

Kayak race at Bellingham Bay.

I live at the edge of Bellingham Bay, the north gate to the greater Puget Sound. Countless kayak put-in sites are scattered along its shores. The bay is heaven for paddlers wishing to explore the rocks and coves along its shores or to cross the expanse of waters to any of the San Juan Islands.

The Nooksack River and other streams empty into this bay forming shallow mudflats and lagoons. Chuckanut Bay—the natives' name for "a bay within a bay"—is Bellingham Bay's jewel, with its coves and rocky bluffs towered with trees. The bay can be calm or gusty and squally. It is my backyard anytime, come rain or sunshine.

It takes about 25 minutes to get to Gooseberry Point from downtown Bellingham. It was dawn in the first week of May, and I was driving toward my put-in at the Point. It was a misty but promising calm day. Cruising slowly west on Marine Drive I pondered about the timing of the morning tides and currents at the western tip of Hale Passage. The plan for the day was to paddle from Gooseberry Point rounding Lummi Island counterclockwise to Lummi Rocks, cross to Eliza Island from Carter Point, skirt Eliza rock and cross Bellingham Bay to South Bellingham at Wildcat Cove, Larrabee State Park, a 16 nautical mile stretch.

The currents can be pretty swift at times over Hale Passage, and in the Georgia and Rosario Straits. "Timing is everything," my father used to say, and indeed it was the key for today. It was almost new moon which means raging currents, so I figured that a fast ride westward will be a nice start.

As the soft music in my car continued to roll I entered Lummi Shore Drive going south and in about seven minutes I reached Gooseberry Point. The Ferry had just arrived from Lummi Island unloading a dozen cars and bikers. I drove my car onto the gravelly parking area near the shoreline. Hale Passage was in a full flood swing. The waves were rolling fast northwest and loud breakers were collapsing onto the shore.

Another kayaker was preparing to launch. We exchanged words about how to time the entrance to the water. "I'm going east, to Inati Bay, I'm not in a hurry," he said softly; "I'll wait a bit for the slack water."

Thirty minutes later, after organizing my gear, I decided to part with him. "Seems that the current is going in my direction, and I'm going to take advantage of it,"

I told him and I shoved my kayak into the flowing current that had weakened a notch. I glided toward the middle of the channel on top of the choppy ripples, quickly passing Lummi Point and venturing on to the open sea where Georgia Strait and Rosario Strait meet at Point Migley.

It was now thirty minutes before the predictable slack, but as I reached the rocks of Point Migley I felt that the ebb current was already there, sucking me toward Rosario Strait. I entered the calm waters between the rocks and the island shoreline where kelp abounds and paddled deeper into the small bay intimating the shoreline.

Seven harlequin ducks and four pigeon guillemots paddled their way toward the big rocks where a black oystercatcher was poking about into a crevice inches above the water line with its gaudy red bill looking for crustaceans or mussels. As I looked ahead, two large seals faced me twenty yards from the bow.

It was somewhat after high tide here and the big rocks were beginning to expose and that's when scores of harbor seals use them as a favorite haul out piazza. These two must have been the forerunners, the ones who would like to get the best view from the top, and they were now following my slow voyage through the kelp, moving from one side of the kayak to the other, exposing their cute faces. As I made some progress south and out of the kelp bed, the seals retreated to the main exposed rock.

Clouds loom over Bellingham Bay.

Rounding Village Point I skidded into the now strengthened ebb current picking up kayak speed and raced joyfully all the way to Baker Reef, three nautical mile distance and a mile short of Lummi Rocks.

The advancing low tide exposed most of the rocks at Baker Reef. The place is majestic. The Lummi Island forested slopes drop abruptly to the shoreline meeting the reef at a narrow strip of gravel beach with tons of dry drifted wood strewn along the tide line. The sun started to penetrate the soft clouds illuminating softly the reef and the exposed beach. The gleaming intertidal rocks reflected a dazzling colorful glow and the beauty was striking.

I wanted to be a part of it, to be absorbed by it, to be eroded into its harmonious spark. Instantly I turned the bow toward the rocks, slowed down to halt and gazed at the beauty as it constantly changed. Finally, I slowly paddled to the east side of the last rock formation composing the reef and landed onto a soft gravelly section of the beach—not far from a lonely bald eagle busy eating on top of a big fish carcass totally ignoring my silent approach. I put my PFD and the skirt on the gravel to dry, sat comfortably on a large log, and eating my tasty rich sandwich I observed the scavenging eagle. For about twenty five minutes the eagle would rip the remains of the fish holding the flesh with its claws. During all of this time the raptor ignored everything else around.

A soft wind started to blow from the southeast rattling the leaves of the bigleaf maple, the ocean spray, and the red alder foliage from the escarpment behind me. By now, bathing in the sun with eyes half closed, enjoying the beauty around me, I was mesmerized by the soft sound of the breaking waves, and the soothing breeze. For me, being all alone, secluded on the edge of a reef, is what kayaking is all about.

Three young gulls landed a few feet from the feasting eagle, screaming, creating a huge commotion, interrupting my peaceful dreams. I was reminded of my itinerary for the day. The eagle didn't move, just gave them his bald eagle look and went on with his meal. I looked at my watch and then examined the flowing ebb current. A long sailboat was cruising south between Orcas and Clark islands three miles away making good progress. It was hard to leave this beach.

Slowly I rolled the kayak into the water and set myself up for Lummi Rocks. After a few strokes I turned the kayak around nosing at the gulls and the eagle. The gulls, in the water now, were fighting and screaming for position, ambushing for the eagle's leftovers. Two more gulls joined the scene, also shrieking for a stake. The eagle, however, was in no hurry.

I wondered why the gulls were even bothering with the eagle and the leftovers. Why spend so much energy? The amount of food material, dead or alive, that was distributed by the action of the tide and the current was enormous. These gulls couldn't be all that hungry. They looked to me full and healthy. And yet, they were burning so much of their energy strategizing a position for the crumbs to be left after the eagle's hopeful departure. Or were they?

Not waiting to see the results of the gulls' contest confrontation, I made progress toward the rocks. Lummi Rocks is a small rocky islet exposed high above the waterline about 150 yards from the island shoreline. At low tide, numerous boulders can be seen encircling the islet and its exposed protected coves and gravelly beaches. The islet is sparsely covered with golden-green grass and flowering annuals.

The ebb current speeded up significantly by now; I paddled closer to the island shoreline outside the strong current, heading toward an inner tiny cove I saw on the northeast side of the islet. A group of

Lummi Rocks is an islet of boulders exposed high above the waterline with numerous small rocks seen only at low tide encircling the main boulders. The shoreline is strewn with small gravelly beaches protected by tiny rugged coves.

harlequin ducks was sunbathing on an elongated exposed rock protected by the passing current examining my slow approach toward the cove. I kept my blades as close to the water as I could so as not to frighten the resting ducks and force them into the moving water.

I rounded the sharp spit of the cove and entered into a pleasant little calm green-blue pool protected perfectly from the Rosario Strait main flow and landed on its intertidal beach. Moving on the wet rocks I climbed onto a grassy knoll for a vista of the whole islet and its shorelines. Just underneath, on an open protected beach, two large California sea lions were napping, taking full advantage of the warming sun while two seals tried to climb onto a ledge not far from where my kayak was anchored.

I was observing the Rosario flow conditions. At the moment it was turbulent but I expected it to subside in thirty minuets or so; I could see the main flow already turning southward, west of Sinclair Island, which meant better paddling conditions along Lummi Island. I gave myself more time out there on the knoll to enjoy the superb view of the San Juan archipelago and the sheer slopes sinking down abruptly from Lummi Peak into the water.

The southern slopes of Lummi and its rugged shorelines are publicly protected as significant core habitats of the marine habitat continuum including a chain of nearby ecologically protected islands along Rosario Strait and the Strait of Georgia. These include eel grass habitats, kelp beds, wetlands, and mature deciduous, evergreen, and coniferous forests. The waterways of the Rosario and Georgia Straits are home to migratory salmon, schools of herring, roaming whales and dolphins like Dall's porpoise, orca, minke, humpback, and gray whales, scores of harbor seals and California and Steller sea lions, and myriad sea birds and raptors. This is a wealth that no sane human can overturn. [Keeping these ecologically productive continuums from high value real estate development will assure rich fauna and flora to last.]

Meanwhile, the sea lions changed their sunbath postures and a great blue heron landed close to the harlequin ducks that were now walking on the wet rocks covered

100

Harbor seals bask on exposed rocks at Lummi Rocks. Harbor seals tend to flee into the water as soon as a sea kayak approaches them closely.

Harlequin ducks and Bonaparte's gulls float leisurely on a drifting log in Bellingham Bay.

in seaweed foraging for aquatic insects, crustaceans, and occasional small fish trapped in shallow pools. The colorful harlequin duck is a diver but will often forage like a plover. A red-throated loon was swimming leisurely close to the cove and four slender pelagic cormorants were flying low in single file, necks outstretched, crossing the channel toward Bellingham Bay.

I set back into my kayak and headed toward Carter Point three nautical miles away enjoying the swift flow of the channel. As I neared the eastern tip of the island, about fifty yards from the rocky point, I

noticed directly in front of me, in a rocky cove, a round glossy hump with a small dorsal fin sticking out of the water. While looking at the approaching wavelets circling toward the port side of the kayak I heard a splash sound and saw a tail fin kicking the water gently and disappearing like it was never there. This was a minke whale, the smallest of the baleen whales roaming the Pacific Northwest waters.

I halted the kayak and stayed afloat for a few minutes gazing around, my heart still pounding, but I didn't see the whale surface again or any sign of it. I had seen minkes in the Puget Sound before, always solitary, always elusive, always for brief moments, but this didn't stop my adrenaline rush following this brief encounter.

I rounded Carter Point and entered a little cove on its northern shoreline. The channel separating Lummi Island and Eliza Island was calm. It was slack time here, and usually this floodless period is brief. I have ridden the swift currents here a few times before, always cautious, respectful, and prepared. This place can be treacherous and should be taken seriously even if it is only a one nautical mile cross. So, without hesitation I crossed the channel to Eliza Island taking advantage of the nice conditions, then skirted Eliza Rock and entered the exceptionally beautiful exposed intertidal zone southeast of Eliza Island for exploration and a rest.

After an hour of wandering on the rocks I pushed myself into Bellingham Bay moving directly east in a waveless sea with a

Wildcat Cove, Larrabee State Park, at low tide.

Sea lions basking in the sun and seals following the kayak's stern are a common sight when kayaking the shorelines of the San Juan Islands.

soft wind in my back toward Wildcat Cove at the Chuckanut mainland, a three nautical mile cross. After a few strokes I assumed a nice paddling rhythm progressing comfortably at around four knots. Chuckanut Mountain with its dense temperate rainforest spread out in front of me in the near distance.

Wildcat Cove, my destination, is nestled just below at the shoreline, protected closely by the sheer Governor Point in the north and Samish Bay waters in the south. The cove is part of Larrabee State Park. Behind Chuckanut Mountain ridge the Cascade foothills rise up tenderly toward the snow-capped Mount Baker and The Sisters. I can see from here only the tips of these peaks. The sun behind me conferred a sharp beautiful green-blue tint to the rainforest cover.

The town of Bellingham is nicely

situated within the rolling foliage hidden in the trees. Today Bellingham metro area is on a fast growth track. The university, the bay, the lush forests and many lakes, the hiking and biking trails, the kayaking routes, the rivers that run through it, the mild weather, and the gateway to the Northern Cascades, San Juan Islands, and British Columbia combined with an unassuming, down-to-earth character are attractive to many people.

As I see it from the kayak, there are still large expanses of open space which I define as core ecological entities intertwined with the urban sprawl. Are these cores safe from development? Can the bay shorelines be protected from massive concrete and steel encroachment? Can the rivers that run through the region continue to transport the vital biotic matter necessary to keep the estuaries, deltas, and intertidal zones alive?

A moderate westerly wind settled in now, giving rise to two-three feet waves. I continuously struck the blades into the

104

The Ski to Sea Race is a major event in Bellingham. Kayakers are waiting for the five mile sea kayak leg.

crested waves to keep the kayak surfing quickly. In fact, it was fun speeding on top of the pushing waves. A trawler, charging fast, passed in front of me making an awfully unorganized sea, forcing me to turn sideway forty-five degrees into the powerful wake and take on the harsh quakes as the kayak crossed through them.

As I was guiding the kayak back to its original course and fun surf I also gained back my thoughts regarding the spatial distribution of the natural green habitats on the mainland just in front of me.

I think the current regional urban growth can be planned more prudently to support sound ecological habitat continuums by interlocking biotic corridors large enough to contain diverse entities like wetlands, tree tops, and complex plant configurations. Proper dispersal of organisms through undisturbed biotic corridors in an urban setting will insure proper ecological productivity and diversity along the regional scale.

Open corridors are good for people too. A maze of hiking trails wriggling through lush ferny and mossy forests, rounding a lake or a pond, or climbing a peak are amenities that people cherish and appreciate. A waterfront easily accessible to paddle watercrafts, with trails for bikes, or for leisurely strolls, a waterfront with vast setbacks from buildings and paved roads are highly valued by people who need these places for fun and relaxation.

When I think about Bellingham I'm referring to a natural unobstructed link between the Nooksack Delta and Samish Bay; a natural connection between Lake Whatcom and the Squalicum Marina, linking the rural areas from Maple Falls to Bellingham town center; and an undeveloped Drayton Harbor and Semiahmoo shorelines. Whatcom County contains the matrix for such networks of biotic corridors. It is the responsibility of its people to define and delineate these links and bond with them in perpetuity.

After sixty minutes of crossing I literally surfed into Wildcat Cove appreciating the madrone trees in full white bloom hanging from the engulfing cliffs enclosing the cove and astounded by the scarlet glow of the tree bark projected by the early evening sun.

The pigeon guillemot is a small alcid seabird, common year round in Washington waters. The birds dive for food close to shores and breed on isolated rocky islands.

9

Sucia Island and Patos Island

Sucia Island, located at the north end of the San Juan archipelago, can be reached by boat only. The Island which is the southern gate to the Strait of Georgia, is a marine state park.

Sucia Island is accessible by boat only. Located at the north end of the San Juan archipelago and at the southern tip of the Strait of Georgia, its shape reminds me of a giant squid moving northwest with the strait current. It is a three hours ride on our *Me Too* trawler going at seven to eight knots from Bellingham. Eva, my wife, and I like to visit Sucia at any given opportunity, but we prefer the spring and fall seasons when it is not overcrowded and when marine wildlife is at its migratory best.

Early in a mid-October morning we loaded *Me Too* with supplies to last us a week, supported the kayak with a few bungee cords on top of the boat's flybridge and, together with our beloved Buddy—our German short-hair pointer—set for Sucia.

Me Too, our marine research vessel, has a nice roomy cabin, a large cockpit, and an open flybridge to observe the surroundings from atop. My preparation for this kayak trip, where the trawler is used as a floating base camp, is obsessively detailed. Tide and current values, marine weather predictions, maps, safety gear, literature, are all stored in my head and on board.

We left Squalicum Harbor around noon and headed toward Hale Passage. Bellingham Bay was calm. The bay is my kayaking backyard. Often I travel along its waterfronts, small bays, coves, and rocks, observing people, boats, wildlife, and the changing weather and seas, especially at day break or sunset, my favorite times of day.

The mountains of British Columbia and the Washington Cascades with Mount Baker's solo peak seemed so close, almost within reach. A group of Dall's porpoises, with dorsal fins barely visible, moved fast along our starboard. Their swift movement was a delight to watch. As we entered Hale Passage, five harbor seals popped up and curiously assessed the approach of the boat. They were hanging in the kelp bed that was moving swiftly with the flood current of the passage.

Harbor seals are common in the bay. Their numbers here are moderate to low. At low tide they haul-out on numerous exposed rocks along the shores of south Bellingham, in Chuckanut Bay, on the eastern shores of Eliza Island, and on Lummi Rocks. Seals are shy on land but very curious in the water when approached by a kayak or a boat. They sniff your stern closely but if you turn to eye them they will disappear instantly.

We now entered the Strait of Georgia waters. The waters were choppy and the moving flood seemed like a surfing zone. Sucia Island was about seven nautical miles away and was visible directly in front of the boat. Pigeon guillemots in small groups were floating gracefully just in front of us. These small solid black sea birds have a pronounced white wing patch and distinct bright red feet. They are members of the auk family and are commonly seen in the sound's protected waters and among its rocks. As we approached them, almost touching, they flew into the air with a sudden shriek, baring their flame-red feet and left into the horizon.

As we approached Matia Island, cruising along its northern rocky shore, we spotted the surprise of the ride: two large flocks, one of cassin's auklets and the other of marbled murrelets, separated by a few yards. I was surprised because I had seen these two pelagic alcid species before in this area but only during the late spring. Passing Matia, we were now entering Echo Bay, where we tied our boat to the state park buoy.

Echo Bay is the largest bay in Sucia and it is protected from southerly and westerly winds. Its mouth is open to the east so it is vulnerable to easterlies. After completing

A fossilized palm tree trunk embedded in the sedimentary rocks of the Chuckanut Formation in a small cove within Chuckanut Bay may indicate a subtropical freshwater habitat in this area ages ago.

the anchoring I slid my kayak into the water, entered it from the swim platform and took off for Ewing Bay, as Eva rowed with Buddy in the dinghy to the nearby shore. The west-northwest shoreline of Echo Bay snakes its length to Ewing Bay.

During low tides I like to enter each of the numerous tiny coves and watch closely the dynamics of the tide pools. The first cove I visited was somewhat wide and rocky with layers of ancient rocks ascending to the tree-carpeted tops. Sucia's rocks store layers of fossil remains of creatures from the distant past which are dated to the Upper Cretaceous era, 81-79 million years ago. These fossils can be easily seen from the kayak.

Sucia Island is thought by current geological theories to be part of a group of islands that may have originated in western Baja California and drifted up the coast to their present position by plate tectonics. Maybe this is why I am so attracted to this spot, which takes me back in time to the days of the Mesozoic Era—the Dinosaurs' Age.

The rocky shore was rich with diverse colors and shapes. Looking up, the branching madrones between the conifer stands engulfed the upper cliff, their reddish bark partly peeled, glaring in the low afternoon sun, outlining the contours of the cliff quite prominently.

Exiting this little bay I zigzagged along the cliffs of various shapes and forms for about a mile. In places the low tide water exposed tiny caves and conglomerates of ancient rocks. I now entered a smaller cove with fine sandstone particles where several juncos were flying low in unison on the exposed beach then disappeared behind tall madrones. The afternoon sunlight gave this small cove a bright Caribbean feel.

The shallow cove was strewn with large eroded boulders resembling an archipelago extending 25-60 yards into the water.

A large group of pelagic cormorants together with a few gulls rested comfortably on the largest boulder. I explored closely these rocks for a while and then continued into Ewing Bay. The entrance to the bay is via a narrow canyon-like shallow channel. The bay is protected on all sides with an opening to the strait the width of a kayak. On the south side there is an extended beach, sandy at low tide, but rocky during high tide.

From previous outings here I realized that this bay is popular for divers looking for crabs. I could kayak in this bay all day

110

Sucia Island is part of a group of islands, the Nanaimo Group, that is thought to have originated in western Baja California and drifted up the Pacific coast to its present location by plate tectonics, the mechanism by which large pieces of the earth's core are broken and travel vast distances over time.

The shoreline of Sucia's Echo Bay snakes its length all the way to Ewing Bay. Kayaking each of the numerous tiny coves is a delight in learning about the past. Along this shoreline layers of fossil remains of creatures from 79-80 million years ago can be seen.

exploring every spot possible. As I turned around and moved forward, facing the opening to the strait, I passed three gulls floating close to a kelp bed. The water was low and the kelp was tight. Dodging within the kelp I made it into the calm and low beefy swells of the Strait of Georgia.

Sucia Island is part of a network of marine park preserves—both in Canada and the US—linked with the mainland through the tidal waters of the Strait of Georgia, Rosario Strait, Haro Strait, and the Strait of Juan de Fuca, and established to ensure its ecological integrity, natural beauty and marine biota diversity. These sensitive habitats also represent myriad places of cultural and spiritual importance to Coast Salish and First Nation tribes on both sides of the border.

However, these waters are constantly affected by habitat disruption and pollution. Shipping activity in the straits of Georgia, Rosario, Haro, and Boundary Pass is heavy, and with it the constant risk of fuel and chemical spills combined with invasion of non-native organisms. The irony here is that although the goal to preserve these ecological entities are commendable, available resources for protection, preservation, and stewardship are in short supply, and often overlooked.

For instance, shoreline sea plants, fish of many species and the orca population are on the decline. But at the same time marine over-exploitation by human activities is remarkably high. In simple terms, the more control humans are gaining on resources, the faster nature is diminishing.

More prudent but also gutsy thinking and actions are necessary. Basically, policies driven by various political motives must be changed drastically towards a comprehensive and more harmonious integration of human and environmental needs.

Looking to the rocks on the north side of my kayak I counted seven harbor seals lying motionless sprawled in different directions. I was motionless and camouflaged in the kelp mass with the paddle rested on the cockpit in front of me, just observing. I was not more than twenty-five yards away from them which was great, since in open waters, free of kelp, I cannot get closer than 100 yards before these beasts dive for safety. The seals were large and full. I moved a bit closer, but this action triggered an instant dive into the water even though they didn't go far. Their heads popped out of the water and curiosity drove them to approach my kayak. A fifteen yard kelp bed separated us.

Five pelagic cormorants returning from their hunt in the open seas landed on the flat boulder freed by the departed seals. I was still in the kelp, making the most of my observation, when I heard a big noise and a splash so familiar to me while kayaking. A huge Steller sea lion male flipped out of the water onto the flat boulder settling itself not far from the cormorants. The sea lion's large neck was adorned by an attractive reddish mane rolling down its chest. It took him a few moments to settle down and be pleased with his special small space. Another group of cormorants arrived, landed, and perched on the remaining space of the flat boulder.

It was sunset and the last vanishing red-orange sun rays projected a bright light on the flat rock with its sea lion, gulls and cormorants forming an amazing array of silhouettes. The light was changing fast and it was time to return to *Me Too*. I knew that the moment I would lift my paddle up and push myself out of the kelp the group of animals in front of me would disappear. With the paddle held low, just inches above the cockpit, I managed to go stern first without causing any commotion and then I slowly returned to Ewing Bay.

I raced back to the boat. After almost three hours in the kayak I needed some exercise. Echo Bay started to fill up with the coming tide. As I was headed west the clouds in the sky changed color from red to dark purple, turning the boats, trees and shoreline into a bizarre display of silhouettes.

112

Massive kelp beds cover the protected waters of the San Juan Islands.

A large great blue heron glided low by my starboard to a nearby roosting spot. When I approached our boat a flock of gulls landed loudly on an elongated dock nearby joining some other gulls for the night, and I realized that the flat rocks outside Ewing Bay, where I had been exploring so extensively twenty minutes ago, were probably covered with tidal water by now forcing the cormorants and gulls to move to their roosting places on higher grounds, and the seals and sea lions to pursue their activities underwater out at sea.

Among the unique features of the waters of the Strait of Georgia surrounding Sucia Island are the multiple directions and speeds of the tidal currents. Predicting tidal current times is difficult and you won't find current speed or direction marks on your nautical maps for this area.

Carefully studying Washburn's tables

A promising landing beach.

114

and some experience is a must for comfort kayaking around here. For instance, just outside Echo Bay, less than a mile out east, ebb current could go in either direction, westward toward Haro Strait, or southeast toward Rosario Strait. It's not until you are in the moving current that you can feel where the water is pushing you. Most of the time you can see from a distance the channel of the moving water zigzagging in wide or narrow bands, but it is hard to detect from your moving kayak its actual direction. In addition, the currents can be fast at times. Ebb speed of 7-10 knots is common. The best time to be out there, therefore, is during slack time, about one hour before or after the changing waters.

But here is why it pays off to be in these unpredictable waters—it is where the most intense marine wildlife activities take place, and all a kayaker has to do is sit still, observe, and delight in this fabulous arena of motion. The unpredictable water behavior here creates humongous densities of plankton life found in the Strait. These look like islands of vegetative masses floating with the currents and wind, or hanging still during slack time and windless periods.

These microscopic masses in turn attract a large array of herbivores and carnivores that roam this sea. It is easy to detect these masses from the kayak by looking for signs of dense floating organic matter, logs, and kelp with flocks of gulls in the water and in the air together with diverse diving waterfowl in one big state of commotion. In my experience kayaking in the Puget Sound and the Inside Passage, such a commotion is a tell-tale sign for underwater feeding activity of marine mammals such as dolphins, whales, or sea lions and seals. The waterfowl species that hover and scream over these masses are in search of food left-overs from the feeding sea mammals.

It was 0530 on a calm, cool, dark morning when I left *Me Too* heading

Rosario Strait waters meet the waters of the Strait of Georgia. These straits are major routes for commercial ships and leisurely travel boats. Sea kayakers should be very cautious in these waters, checking current tables and weather conditions very closely.

115

toward the open waters of the Strait of Georgia. My plan was to spend the early morning hours watching sea animals feed. My strategy was to be out an hour before slack, explore the waters for two or three hours, and then leave just shortly before the maximum current arrives.

As I passed the eastern section of Ewing Bay and entered into the open sea the glowing pink-red sunrise sky was seen behind Mount Baker miles away to the east. The sky was clear, the water was calm as a tabletop, and the air was cold with a thin moving mist. Wearing appropriately warm kayak gear I felt comfortable in the cockpit. It was a slow paddle to observe my immediate surroundings. I was looking for a large concentration of sea birds, afloat or airborne as a sign of sea mammal activity. I was moving now toward the north, about two miles northeast of Patos Island. It was quiet; the only sound I could hear was the sound of the paddle when it hit the water. It was very relaxing.

After about twenty minutes heading north I could detect a bulk of floating kelp and plankton mass 200 yards in front of the kayak. Sea gulls were circling the kelp area with the familiar noise of excitement. Getting closer I could see on my port side two seals poke their heads out of the water towards me. I moved closer, and about 50 yards from the floating kelp, I saw an area the size of a football field of murky waters filled with bubbles and foam. Sea gulls, pigeon guillemots, and a group of surf scoters circled the site. The sea gulls were going nuts making noisy grunts, diving and screaming as if a loaded fishing boat were around getting rid of unwanted fish.

I knew right then and there that something was happening down underwater. I stopped the kayak and searched with my binoculars the area with the bubbles. Nothing. I sat and waited. Two more seals were facing me from the starboard and behind. The morning light was enhanced by the rising sun. Two pacific loons swam calmly not far from the kayak. Suddenly, I heard an abrupt splashy sound just short of my bow, as if water were exploding under my kayak. Following the splash two whale

heads appeared right in front of me, with their mouths ajar, breaching out vertically in a spiral and diving sideways knocking down the water surface with their flippers as they disappeared. Wow! Humpbacks.

I could not believe the moment. My adrenalin was pumping. I was tightening my thighs which were pushing against the cockpit, holding firmly my paddle at water level. I was too close to the whales' feeding grounds. These huge mammals were no joking matter here in the middle of their feast. I paddled backwards, twenty-thirty yards away from the concentrated mass and foamy waters, focusing on the stability of the kayak.

Then, with a booming sound, the two whales were out again, breaching low, heads up and sideways, mouths open wide, holding this pose for a moment before disappearing, this time further away from me. Small waves were pushing the kelp toward the kayak. The birds were all over the area. It was like a huge party. Hungry sea gulls soared and dodged inches above the water pecking at one another, aiming for bits of floating silver colored fish. I was trying to reach for my camera, but hesitated. There is no way I could handle the paddle and the camera at the same time, let alone take a snapshot. I had to be on the alert.

Although I wanted to be as close as I could near the feeding action, the commotion was too big and it was probably less safe there. A small kelp bed floated to my port.

116

I penetrated the kelp bed and anchored my kayak in the middle of the heavy plant mass for stability. Now was a "sit and wait" time. I was quiet and patient but exuberant and excited. The bubbles were still active. The size of the feeding site was even larger now.

Three to five minutes passed by and I could feel from the water around me that the humpbacks were not yet done eating. And then there was another strike. This time it was 100 yards to the east. Only one whale was seen out breaching vertically with its right whitish-gray flipper hanging momentarily in the air before splashing the water. No sooner did this whale disappear,

leaving behind a trail of bubbles, than another whale popped out of the water, mouth open, just in front of my eyes.

This was incredible. I could not identify what these whales preyed upon because the waters were way too bubbly. I reached my bottle of water and drank. A few moments later the gulls' noise was diminishing. I was still within the kelp bed, believing it was safe there.

Humpbacks are enormous baleen whales belonging to the Rorqual family. They possess baleen plates that are attached to their upper jaws which function as filters screening food particles immersed in the

The Orca whales circle the San Juan archipelago via Haro Strait, Boundary Pass, and Rosario Strait in pursuit for food year round. Three known pods of resident orcas and a number of transient groups are known to inhabit these waters. Transients and residents have different feeding preferences: The former prey on small and large sea mammals, while the latter eat mainly fish.

water entering their mouth. Humpbacks feed on schooling small fish like herrings, krill, small thumb-size crustaceans, and microscopic plankton. They feed by lunging forward at the surface or by rushing to their prey from below. They deploy large bubble nets around a school of fish or krill swarms, trapping their prey for an easy grab. To do this the humpbacks form a circle underwater then force air out through their blowholes as they ascend to the surface creating a net of bubbles and then they surface openmouthed right where the concentrated mass of prey is.

118

It is reported that between two and more than a dozen individuals participate in this type of communal lunge creating bubbles, deploying flipper beating, and using sounds. They are seasonal feeders, eat only during the summer and fall months, when they spend their time in the cold water, away from their warm-water breeding grounds. During feeding days an individual whale

Observing wildlife from a sea kayak is a delight.

consumes more than one ton per day of plankton, small fish, and krill.

The only other time I was lucky to observe the humpbacks' cooperative feeding was in Fife Sound just southwest of the Burdwood Group and Raleigh Passage where I was kayaking solo the Queen Charlotte Strait and the Broughton archipelago, British Columbia, in July of 2002. It was around 4:30 AM on a cool, misty to light rain morning. The Sound was calm and quiet and I was paddling slowly, exploring, when I heard the continuous sounds of whale air blows and splashes about 200 hundred yards to my port. Humpbacks, at least five of them, were seen surfacing tails up, circling a small area, diving and breaching vertically, and making tremendous commotion.

As I moved a bit closer, I could see clearly three large mouths open widely as they poked out of the water. For ten minutes these humpbacks were splashing vigorously in the waters. I sat there, in my cockpit, amazed by the enormous energy exerted by these whales as they dived into the water while at the same time engaging in such delicate, subtle spiral motion as they torpedoed out. It was surreal. Here I was, alone, in the middle of a remote and vast waterway, in light rain and mist, in the midst of an enormous activity performed by several hundred tons of whale energy totally ignoring me, and I was so tiny, so insignificant.

Following heavy rains water cascades through the vegetated cliffs of the Sucia Island shorelines.

Several minutes passed by and nothing was happening. A large fishing boat was approaching from the east directly toward my position. I was getting ready to move to the open to let the boat see me. It was near 0800. The current was picking up and I could see the kelp mass with all its murky water moving steadily as one unit gaining momentum by the minute. By the time the wake of the passing fishing boat hit my kayak the feeding site became quiet; only a few gulls stayed behind poking around, but otherwise it seemed that the humpbacks' feeding episode was over. The humpbacks were gone, vanished without a trace.

I circled the area for few more minutes and then turned west and paddled into Echo Bay. I was elated. The rare opportunity I had experienced minutes ago witnessing from close distance two humpback whales in their feeding pursuits was unsurpassed.

Although I had been looking forward

to observe sea animals in action I had never dreamed to encounter those humpbacks feed right here three nautical miles from my put-in. As I approached *Me Too,* with Eva and Buddy on board, the air around was filled with the aroma of fresh coffee, announcing the start of a new day.

The next day I started my paddling late, at around 11 AM, leaving Eva painting on the boat's deck with Buddy asleep by her side. My plan was to explore the Sucia southwest shores and then kayak to Patos Island, which is a little more than two nautical miles from the northwest portion of Sucia Island. Crossing the waters to Patos Island from Sucia needed to be close to slack, which was to happen in the afternoon. Although the tidal changes for the day were predicted to be small I wanted to play it safe.

The water was glossy flat, and the cool air stood still with no wind. I was heading toward Johnson Point at the southeast tip of the Sucia fingers. The bay was deserted from people and boats. I was alone, paddling slowly, and comfortable in the cockpit enjoying the sound of the water. Kayaking through the narrow passage between two of the numerous fingers in this group of islands I thought to myself how fortunate I was to be in this quiet, peaceful moment where the only sounds coming to my ears were my paddle breaking the water and the vibrations of the kayak as it sliced the waterway. Allan Watts' words came to mind, "Just observe and relax and live the brief moment. Just let your eyes see whatever they see and let it go: do not force your breath."

As I looked to my left and my right at the dense vegetation towering the cliffs and sedimentary rocks, I tried to imagine myself floating back in time together with the island from its original location ages ago somewhere within the 25-degree parallel of Baja California. Geologists and paleontologists are still debating the age and fate of these isolated small islands east of Vancouver Island named the Nanaimo Group.

The use of geomagnetic polarity techniques delivered some convincing evidence that these small islands originated as a result of an explosive tectonic plate collision at the 25 parallel and floated through time alongside the isolated Vancouver Island to their present locations. In fact, according to recent seismic signs, the islands are still on the move—about two centimeters a year in a northwest direction.

With the enormous changes that have occurred since the mass extinction at the end of the Mesozoic Era, I knew that I would probably not see today any sea reptiles, dinosaurs, or live gigantic clams and ammonites, but I thought I would be just as content to encounter a number of sea anemones, giant octopuses, and sea stars grazing the intertidal zones of rocks

From early October hundreds of western grebes roam the protected waters of the San Juan archipelago where they winter. This elegant grebe is extremely vulnerable to human disturbance like oil spills, gill nets, and poisons.

and pools, or a bald eagle soaring the open water of a small bay, or maybe even sea lions and big whales roaming for food along this journey. Apart from the difference in time scale, the Sucia waterways are still a floating museum of the past.

A family of river otters diving for fish brought me back. They were about 50 yards away from my port using a deep tide pool in a tiny cove just off the tip of South Finger Island. I tucked my kayak behind an extended rock, and blending with the cliff, I watched these shy acrobatic mammals in their brisk bustle in pursuit of food. I could count five otters: two adults and three young. They dived along the cliffs and soon re-emerged with their long white-gray whiskers followed by a mouthful of fish. One of the adults climbed on a small flat boulder to handle its extra large catch which must have

Patos Island is a marine state park. At the Toe Point area the shoreline is rugged and the intertidal zone is extensive and full of life forms.

been too difficult to handle in the water. Then as soon as it consumed its prey, it zoomed back into the water for more. After a few minutes of fishing, the group settled on a flat rock, where the adults busied themselves grooming while the young played in and out of the water, tangling together on shore and splashing in the water.

These otters show amazing maneuverability. The northern river otter is a common predator in the San Juan archipelago and can be seen regularly in Sucia. This elongated, slender, webbed-foot swimmer differs markedly from the larger mustelid northern sea otter of which there have been no recent observations in this area. While the sea otter spends its time in the water swimming, feeding, and napping on its back, rarely using land, the river otter, although well adapted to its aquatic life, is also a terrestrial creature.

I continued alongside the shore, circled Johnson Point, and entered into Snoring Bay. The water was calm and quiet. A mature bald eagle perched on a large madrone branch was studying my activity.

Its head moved slowly, from side to side as I paddled. A group of harlequin ducks, in tight formation, moved slowly into Fossil Bay when I crossed the entrance. As I skirted the south cliffs two black oyster-catchers were chiseling the rocks at water-line with great pertinacity using their long sharp reddish beaks in pursuit of thin-shelled limpets and mussels.

From here, for about two miles west-ward, the gravelly-rocky beaches are like a floating museum from the past—the sheer cliffs expose ancient layers of rocks. Starting with the oldest layer closest to the waterline,

each successive layer tells a detailed account of the sedimentary rock strata of Fossil Bay as so richly described by Peter Ward, a pale-ontologist, in his book *Time Machine*.

I took my time exploring these walls of natural history and started day-dreaming again, imagining enormous sea reptiles roaming here 80 millions years ago biting with their sharp hammer-like jaws on diverse fish species and ammonites, maybe climbing onto the shallow shore for short visits of egg deposits, then vanishing into extinction 65 millions years ago by the colli-sion of a giant comet with the earth, to be

123

Landing at Patos Island.

replaced by the gigantic baleen and toothed whales of today. I closed my eyes. Hearing the sounds of the small surf breaking onto the ancient beach transformed my soul back in time where I could clearly see those giant mosasaurs of the Cretaceous period circling my kayak. It was a profound experience intensified by the silence of the moment with no one to interrupt my wild imaginations.

It was now a little over two hours since I entered the water. A few hundred feet from my port side I noticed some signs of organic murk floating steadily westward, indicating the direction of the current as I was passing by Parker Reef. Reaching Shallow Bay, I angled the kayak northwest and initiated the cross to Toe Point at Patos Island about two miles away over the windless flat and glossy waters at fast speed. In the distance I saw a fishing boat working its way west, encircled by a noisy crowd of sea gulls and cormorants.

Patos is a small island at the north end of Boundary Pass. It belongs to the same chain of islands that originated in Baja. Wild, peaceful, and isolated, it is a marine state park not frequently busy with people.

124

Camping on Posey Island.

Kelp beds are numerous along the Strait of Juan de Fuca and Haro Strait where migrating salmon take refuge, and seals, sea lions, and whales play and prey.

As I was approaching the south shore of the island, I could clearly see the cliffs and bluffs made of conglomerate rocks similar to Sucia's. The Toe Point area—a marvelous intertidal zone to explore with the kayak at low tides—was partially exposed.

Two adult bald eagles perched on a tall conifer tree took off and soared low in front of me as I entered the cove. This area along with the southern vegetated bluffs is a large bald eagle nesting habitat designated as a Heritage Area by the state to be enjoyed from a distance. The eagles made a few circles inside the cove and landed on the exposed tidal rocks at the west corner of the cove.

I left the cove and the eagles alone, and entered an adjacent cove littered with rocks of different shape and size. The rocky outcrops were massive, and it was therefore no wonder that I encountered a group of harbor seals, seven in number, who splashed vigorously into the water as soon as they detected me.

The kelp bed was so dense here that I could hear the sound of the kelp heads crashing into my kayak. Some of the seals stuck their heads just above the kelp surface making it hard to tell them apart from the kelp heads.

Just as I was rounding the outer rocks toward the next cove and into a nice sandy

Prevost Harbor, Stuart Island. Although scattered with private homes and boat docks, Stuart Island is still remote. For kayakers its coves and inlets are heaven where encounters with diverse wildlife is at its best.

beach I heard the sound of a low pitched, sneeze-like air blow, coming from the direction of my starboard. I waited for a while. Moments later I could hear another air blow. This time I could see an elongated dark body with a small dorsal fin and an elevated forked tail fin. I froze and looking around, waited for something to happen. Seconds later there was another blow, this time about 20 feet in front of my kayak. The whale surfaced again, this time turning sideways to its right, exposing parts of its left black and white flipper and its whitish underside with its mouth and eye submerged in the bubbling water. The mammal then disappeared without leaving a trace. This was a lone minke whale. I have encountered minkes before, but I have never seen them perform a side flop. This was pretty incredible.

The Haro Strait waterway is threatened by pollutants questioning the health of its diverse biota. Although sea kayaking is still a pleasure here, no one knows for how long people and governments can control its ecological integrity.

Minke whales are common in the channels of the San Juan Islands. They are baleen and the smallest of the rorquals. Still, they can get to 35 feet in length and weigh close to 12 tons, so these are by no means small beasts. Although they spend only little time close to the water surface, I frequently spot them close to kelp beds in shallow waters. Many a time, they are associated with crowded waterfowl seeking food within murky slow moving currents. This whale was once heavily hunted; but today, international regulations protect this baleen in its range. In the Pacific Northwest the minke population is on the rise.

In less than a mile I approached Alden Point with its beautiful light house. The point terrain is the only bare land on the island which is otherwise densely vegetated. As I circled the point I entered into a corridor of tidal rips. These are always on the move.

With the low tide running I crossed the

50-70 yard-wide rippling corridor pushing my bow with the rushing waves about 45 degrees toward the south shore nearby. This was fun. I could do it over and over, catching the noisy water.

The cliffy, bare wall of the south shore is the entrance to Active Cove, a narrow channel between Patos Island and Little Patos Island. A bald eagle perching on an exposed large rock by the waterline inspected me as I entered the narrow channel. Not far from there, a colorful great blue heron waded slowly in a shallow vegetated rocky pool stretching its neck as I passed by. The cove was free of boats, and I landed on the partly exposed sandy beach, by the state park camp site.

128

Around 4 PM I set off back to Sucia Island. The water was calm, with a cool soft breeze blowing from the southwest. I wandered a little eastward along the south shore observing the ancient sedimentary rocks. Two seals followed me into the cove and out.

I pointed the kayak toward Shallow Bay easily seen in the distance, and speeded up my pace maintaining constant rhythm. About half way into the channel I passed a bunch of waterfowl congregated by a massive bed of sea weed and kelp. Even though I didn't interrupt my fast pace I could identify scoters, murrelets, pigeon guillemots, grebes, and gulls. They were all relaxed, seemingly moving with the wind to nowhere. In the distance, to the west, I could hear a number of whale blows.

It is amazing how many different sounds you can hear at a moment of listening, but somehow, I always try to filter out what they are, who they belong to, and where they come from. I often wish I could follow Allan Watts' advice when he said, "as the sounds fade away transformed to all other noises do not ask yourself what the sound is, or what it means, just hear it and dig it."

The sun was low by now, and Shallow Bay with its rocky narrow entrance was magnificent. Two boats tied to buoys created a sense of home. Eva, with Buddy on leash, strolled on the beach waving loudly toward me as I sliced the kayak into the sand. It was great to be back with my loved ones.

THREE

Olympic Coast Watersheds – Pacific Ocean

Boundary Pass and its connecting waters are constantly affected by habitat disruption and pollution. Shipping activity is on the rise and with it the constant risk of fuel and chemical spills combined with invasion of non-native organisms.

The Elwha River mouth is narrow at its opening to the Strait of Juan de Fuca.

10

Elwha River to Crescent Bay

Black oystercatchers and a friend.

In late October around noon I entered the Elwha River from its east bank, about quarter of a mile from the river's mouth where it empties into the Strait of Juan de Fuca. The weather was cool, partly cloudy, and windless. The muddy beach is a launching site for small motorized boats used mainly by fishermen of the local Elwha tribal people.

Actually, my initial intention was to start my exploration further upriver below the Elwha Dam, but the course there was too shallow and rocky to negotiate a sea kayak. Although the water level was on the rise in that section of the river, the tidal changes today were negligible. While the west bank is mostly a shoal with a sharply exposed spit, the east bank is densely vegetated and marshy.

As I was settling comfortably into the cockpit, a group of common goldeneye guided me into a wide entrance to a marshy area to the east. This small slough, protected by the elevated bay shoreline, branches into small channels, which are loaded with waterfowl; but unfortunately, these channels are too small for kayak explorations.

The constant sound of the breaking waves outside this enclosed shallow estuary hinted at what was coming in the open sea just yards away. On the shore of a tiny islet a bald eagle was busy tearing apart a large salmon carcass while two gulls were hovering above the raptor screeching at each other. As I approached the scene the eagle gathered the fish remains with its talons and took off to a sandy ridge at the bay shoreline, followed by the hungry gulls.

Returning to the river, I slowly approached the narrow opening to Freshwater Bay to assess my options to paddle in the open waters.

The Elwha River collects its water from the western flanks of West Peak and Chimney Peak and the eastern slopes of Mount Christie, Mount Seattle, Mount Queets, and Mount Barnes, and from the north and east slopes of Bailey Range, all

are within Olympic National Park. It then flows north for forty miles into Freshwater Bay in the Strait of Juan de Fuca, at Angeles Point.

Since 1900 the Elwha River water flow has been regulated by two dams: Glines Canyon Dam which created Lake Mills, and Elwha Dam which formed Lake Aldwell. These two dams are expected to be removed by 2010, enforced by the Elwha River Ecosystem and Fisheries Restoration Act of 1992. The dismantled dams will bring the river to its original flow pattern from mountains to sea without interruptions. The free and fast flowing Elwha will eventually restore the salmon habitats and runs. In addition, it will most likely also alter the topography and ecology of the river's mouth as seen today, by active sediment transport and deposits.

Gliding along the west shore of the river mouth I faced two-to-three foot waves that exploded at the shallows to my starboard, but the deeper channel to my port close to the west spit was smooth and surf free. In a few more strokes I passed the surf zone and paddled gently onto the beefy, long, three foot swells, outside Freshwater Bay. It was now more than one hour past the predicted slack time. The maximum ebb current was expected in two more hours.

Just looking toward the swells of the vast body of water in front of me, thinking about the powerful and intense water motion of the Strait gave me an adrenalin

Calm dawn at the Strait of Juan de Fuca.

132

The Elwha River originates from the northern slopes of Olympic National Park, emptying its waters into the Strait of Juan de Fuca at Freshwater Bay. The river's flow and level are controlled by two dams expected to be dismantled by 2010, bringing the river to its original uninterrupted flow from the mountains to the sea. A free fast flow will eventually restore forgotten salmon habitats

rush, which put me in my zone. After all, I was kayaking the Strait of Juan the Fuca, the sole channel linking the immense deltas of the Northern Cascades rivers with the vast Pacific Ocean.

Although the current at the moment was less than one knot, I felt the drifting northwest, especially as I paused for a photo snap. The wind picked up a little since I entered the Elwha River. A large group of surf and white-winged scoters was rolling the swells just outside Angeles Point as I changed direction westward.

Some drifting wood and kelp were scattered in front of my course. Ahead, two common loons were taking note of my movement and in the far distance I saw a fishing boat leaving Freshwater Bay. Otherwise I was alone on the surface of this gigantic moving body of water. Vancouver Island to the north was barely visible. The rugged peaks of the Olympic range to the south were majestic in the mixture of gray clouds and blue skies. In less than an hour I reached Observatory Point on the west side of Freshwater Bay and landed on a rocky beach dense with kelp and enclosed by large boulders with gnarled madrone trees hanging on top. A narrow cave with a lively western red cedar in front greeted me as I landed in this perfect spot. The time was nearing the predicted maximum ebb current and I thought I could wait here for the current at the Strait to diminish in strength.

The Strait of Juan de Fuca is a gateway to enormous water forces which push their gigantic way to and from the Pacific Ocean: waters drain from the Northern Cascades Mountains of British Columbia and Washington, from the northern slopes of the Olympic range, and from the southern slopes of the Vancouver Island mountains. These mixed with sea water by the tidal

forces, move in two colossal ebb cycles twice in twenty four hours via the narrow channel of the Strait of Juan de Fuca between Cape Flattery, Washington, and Carmanah Point, Vancouver Island, BC, a narrow gap of 19 nautical miles.

These are the water forces that help maintain the vast deltas of the Fraser, Nooksack, Samish, Skagit, Snohomish, Sammamish, Green, Nisqually, and Elwha rivers. The Strait of Juan de Fuca is also the main shipping channel linking the Pacific Ocean with the ports of Vancouver, BC, Bellingham, Padilla Bay, Everett, Seattle, Tacoma, Olympia, Port Angeles and Victoria, BC. Gigantic commercial oil tankers and freighters move daily carrying oil to the refineries and other goods to

Kayaking with the orca is an exhilarating experience.

The east entrance to Crescent Bay, Strait of Juan de Fuca.

destinations around the world. Oil and toxic spills from these carriers are common occurrences. Tidal currents move the oil muck into bays, inlets, and river deltas within these areas. Millions of dollars flow annually into programs to protect from oil spills and cleaning.

It was time to leave.

I rounded Observatory Point heading west gliding on top of three-foot beefy swells about 150 yards away from the rugged shoreline. I kept thinking about the magnitude of the water pushing me west and the ecology along this magnificent channel. Cold Pacific water is driven by rising tides into the Juan de Fuca, mixing along its way east with warmer waters along the bays and inlets, and then rebounding back toward the ocean during ebb tides, creating in the process ecological conditions that support a great number of habitats and diverse organisms.

Unfortunately, today all of these habitats are highly contaminated with pollutants which affect harvestable species making them unfit for human consumption. The Strait of Juan the Fuca is on one hand an important biological corridor bridging sea waters and fresh waters, but on the other

Salt Creek empties its waters into the east side of Crescent Bay forming a beautiful estuary. Exposed boulders are constantly eroded by the actions of surging waves and strong winds. Rounding the rocks at Tongue Point and entering the estuary in a sea kayak can be done in calm seas.

136

hand, it is also a major reservoir for toxins emitted from the compact urban life.

Toxic pollutants are not the only cause for marine life depletions; extensive timber harvest along these productive waterfronts is another reason for the ecological deterioration of the straits and the sounds. The enormous land sweep seen by forest removal, roads, and building site excavations in turn produce major erosions and slope slides. The eroded particles flood down unchecked, sometimes at accelerating speed, to be deposited in eddies along creeks and rivers, and in river deltas, changing constantly riparian and estuarine habitats.

The rate of the ebb current began to diminish as I made progress toward Tongue Point, which was still two miles away. The rugged shoreline with its caves and grottos was impressive. Actually, at this point I was galloping on top of an elaborate reef, which was partly exposed near the shore. This section and all the way to Tongue Point, well known to be an outstanding intertidal ecosystem, had been designated as a Marine Life Sanctuary years ago.

As I neared the point, the kelp became thickly bedded providing me some anchoring for photo-taking and bird and seal sighting. A few people were walking along the exposed rocks by the beach of Salt Creek Park examining the colorful intertidal marine organisms. It seems that people are eager to visit such places and watch the rich floral and faunal life so carefully preserved here. But I wondered… for how long?

Slowly I reached Tongue Point, the entrance to Crescent Bay. I paused momentarily within the kelp to assess my maneuvers around the exposed boulders knifing out there. The coming waves washed these rocks and then rebounded in all possible directions. While I was waiting on the swells watching the surf I heard repeated whale blows not far away. Looking closely toward the familiar sound I saw three large tail fins just yards from my starboard.

Definitely gray whales, as judged by the unmistakable odor from the splashed spray, blown to my face. The leviathans were moving west. They were most likely the last individuals leaving Puget Sound to join other grays on their winter migration south to the warmer waters of Baja California.

Whales are still frequenting Puget Sound and the surrounding straits and sounds. I'm curious for how long they will continue to roam in these waters during the summer months looking for viable food. With the ceaseless depletion of micro and macro flora and their accompanying zooplankton and fish on which the whales depend for food, there will soon be a time when these unique creatures will stop venturing into these waters. Orca and humpback are already showing signs of number reduction.

I decided to round the exposed rocks away from the surf and enter the mouth of Salt Creek from the west where the bay looked calm. As I resumed my course, two California sea lions coming from the west passed close to my port and disappeared to Tongue Point on the east side. A few sea gulls were standing on the rocks west to the point braving the surf. I headed toward the mouth of Salt Creek, rounding from the west a tall rocky islet covered with a few trees on top where the unbroken waves were small and friendly enough to surf me into the creek's beautiful channel.

Dodging between floating logs the creek curved to the right, touching shallow waters close to a spit where I reached the grassy bank by the public parking area and landed safely shortly before the fading sun glow disappeared for the night.

138

The rock formation at the Olympic Coast is astounding—adorned with caves, arches, and sheer lushly vegetated cliffs rising abruptly from the shoreline. It is a place where the sea otter finds its safe haven and ample food.

11

Neah Bay to Makah Bay

Tatoosh Island. The Strait of Juan de Fuca meets the Pacific Ocean here.

In late September, just before daybreak, I settled in my kayak on the beach by the breakwater at the southwest corner of Neah Bay. It was a quiet, windless morning; the Strait of Juan de Fuca was peaceful and glossy. A thin layer of a silvery cloud formation with a flat, gloomy grayish hue was reflected on the soundless passage.

The mountain ridges on Vancouver Island in the distance to the north were still shrouded in dim light. I thought to myself: I hit the jackpot; the entrance to the strait was bound to stay calm all day, and not much would be going on weather-wise in the Pacific Ocean as well. It is risky and unwise to kayak the entrance area of the Strait when the sea is high, windy, and large swells collide brutally ashore.

My plan was to kayak along the south shoreline of the Strait of Juan de Fuca to its entrance, round Cape Flattery, enter the Pacific Ocean, and land at Makah Bay on Hobuck Beach. Today was my window of opportunity to calmly explore this remarkable and splendid shoreline. This stretch of convoluted coastline, parts of which are within Flattery Rocks National Wildlife Refuge and the Olympic National Park, is one of the most spectacular in the Pacific Northwest.

Sea weeds and clusters of giant kelp carpeted my pathway outside this reef. I had to clear the track with my fingers, pushing the horizontally floating flora aside; the paddle was too large to fit the job. High tide was in progress and was predicted to culminate around 9:40 AM, when I would be close to Tatoosh Island about six miles away, if all went according to plan. Most importantly, the ebb current at the channel would begin only in two hours and it was predicted to be less than one knot at its maximum in the Strait entrance by noon.

As I approached Koitlah Point, about half a mile into my paddle, I noticed some white splashes at the exposed rocks that line the entrance to the bay I was in. As I rounded the Point and entered the Juan de Fuca I was greeted by three-foot-high beefy, organized swells which had been obscured from the beach when I put in. Ostensibly, I was expecting a slight sweep toward the east, but in reality I witnessed a drag westward.

Keeping my path outside the main kelp blanket I galloped along the reef line over to Chibahdehl Rocks. At times, I mistakenly took the large, partially submerged, gas-filled bulbs of the floating bull kelps for seal heads popping out of the water staring at me. But a closer look revealed the elaborate blades attached to the long beefy stem-like stipe. These substantial masses of kelp can reduce the hydrodynamic forces of the incoming swell and thus become a safe haven for a moving kayak, but when encountered floating singly in a swell they can be dangerous for their impact on a moving kayak.

After rounding Slant Rock I moved into a large bay with many coves and eddies along a remarkably rugged shoreline. The water in the bay was calm and the swells unnoticeable. I dodged between the kelp stems that were actually protecting me, and stirred my way closer to the partially exposed reef. I was nearing high tide and the water level was fairly high here.

It was tempting to go ashore and walk along the tide pools and the small stretch of the sandy beach for a while, but time was precious now; I still had to round the cape and this had better be done before the arrival of maximum ebb.

I reached a small cove extending west to Mushroom Rock and anchored into a motionless thick kelp bed for scouting. This place provided me with an excellent view of Tatoosh Island, the entrance into Juan de Fuca, and the passage between Cape

140

The Neah Bay's convoluted coastline is one of the most spectacular in the Pacific Northwest. Parts of it are within Flattery Rocks National Wildlife Refuge and the Olympic National Park.

Flattery and Tatoosh Island. The site was amazing in its beauty: The rock formation was adorned with caves and arches and the lushly vegetated sheer cliffs rose straight from the shoreline. The steady rhythmic soft sound produced by the waves as they splashed on the exposed rocks was reciprocated by the booming sounds emanating from the nearby hollow cavities of the tall caves when the swells hit their inner walls providing an atmosphere of calm and peacefulness.

Bull kelps proliferate on rocky shores with abundant nutrients, tidal motion, and cool clear sea water. It is an annual brown algae which grows to its full massive size by late summer and early fall. The bulb which buoys the blades to the surface for photosynthesis contains a mixture of gasses. The long stipe, or the stem-like structure, is attached to a holdfast that anchors the brown algae to a rock or the sea floor. The wave-swept kelps support a diverse array of organisms. They provide feeding and rest for sea urchins, rockfish, fin fish, juvenile salmons, waterfowl, shorebirds, and marine mammals to name a few. In addition, masses of kelp soften the force of incoming waves against the shoreline, and thus help in markedly reducing shoreline erosion.

For a sea kayaker at times of turbulent seas, the kelp can be a temporarily safe haven. But, most importantly to a kayaker at sea, the kelp is useful in predicting the direction and speed of tidal currents by the alignment of the floating algae. When current rates are slow, kelp floats horizontally, with the stipe flat on the water surface. When the current accelerates, the stipe submerges and the kelp moves vertically with its bulb popping out of the water. Keen observation and experience will help determine the stipe position relative to the moving water and thus its direction and speed.

From the comfort of the kelp bed in the cove, I assessed the current situation. I noticed a mild current entering the 1.5-mile long and 0.7-mile wide channel between Tatoosh Island and Cape Flattery rocks coming from the northeast. Small tidal ripples quivered along the passage, but otherwise the waterway seemed comfortably calm. It was nine thirty, more than two hours before the current would reach its

highest speed. I decided to stay away from the shores of Tatoosh Island and paddle closer to the Cape's sea stacks directing my bow toward the southwest side of Jones Rocks, where the opening to the ocean appeared moderately calm, thus avoiding the incoming waves to the coves and tiny fjords of Cape Flattery.

As I was skirting the waters I was accompanied by flocks of sea gulls and pigeon guillemot. Five curious harbor seals peeked at me from my starboard, hesitant to flee. As I got closer to Jones Rocks I heard the growl of sea lions from the direction of the island. I slowed down bracing the kayak to face Tatoosh, and, sure enough, saw four large Steller sea lions basking on a large flat boulder. I took that opportunity to look at the Tatoosh Island lighthouse standing firm above the cliffy slope.

The entrance to the Strait of Juan de Fuca between Tatoosh Island and Vancouver Island spans nineteen miles. Here is where the bulk of the tidal currents change direction. Fresh waters from the rivers and runoffs that enter Puget Sound, the Strait of Georgia, and the Strait of Juan de Fuca mix with salt water coming from the ocean in a turbulent exchange of nutrients, minerals, and chemical compounds.

Here is where adult salmon enter in order to reach their spawning habitats up the rivers and mountain creeks and where yearling salmon, after acclimating to the salt water of the Strait, leave for the open

142

Cape Flattery caves.

ocean. Here is where pods of whales enter and leave in their search for food. Likewise, here is the main entrance to the Strait for commercial and pleasure transportation fleets visiting the ports along its shores. The strait is very much alive.

I skirted James Rocks and entered the Pacific Ocean.

I reached the open sea and was greeted by a southerly wind whipping up three-to-four foot swells. I was thrilled. I have accomplished my goal of paddling rivers, bays, sounds, and straits all the way from the mountains to the Pacific Ocean.

Rounding James Rocks I steered southward closer to the serrated, rugged coastline just outside the surf. On the north side of Fuca Pillar—a group of sharply posing sea stacks resembling a Stonehenge shrine—I noticed some movement between the rocks. When I moved closer I was pleasantly surprised to discover three sea otters eagerly

Cape Flattery fjords scattered with sea stacks.

144

active, sharing the spot with a lonely harbor seal. The otters dived and disappeared the second they noticed me despite the distance between us. This was my first encounter with sea otters along the Washington coast.

Sea otters had been extirpated off the coast of Washington by fur traders late in the 19th century. In the early seventies of the 20th century a new population, totaling fifty-nine individuals, was established by translocation from Alaska. As of 2008, the population has been estimated at around 800 individuals roaming the rocky reefs from Destruction Island in the south to Cape Flattery in the north. Some sea otters ventured lately into the reef habitats along the Strait of Juan de Fuca and two or three were sighted in the south Puget Sound.

The preferred food of the sea otter, among other subtidal invertebrates, is sea urchins. Because of their high metabolic needs, mainly to keep their body temperature in check, the sea otters have to consume about 25 percent of their body weight, translating into 15-20 pounds of food daily. They dive for prey almost constantly, groom their fur for hours, and rest briefly within dense kelp beds. They feed, rest, and raise their young exclusively in the water, rarely landing on hard surfaces. I spent some time searching for the otters but to no avail.

Rounding the second set of the Fuca Pillar rocks I entered into an expansive calm bay where I could paddle much closer to the exposed section of the reef and look for sea otters. Midway into the bay I sighted a group of river otters diving and splashing furiously within a deep tidepool enclosed by large rocks, ignoring my presence as I paddled through.

At Waatch Point two Steller sea lions resting on a flat low boulder raised their upper body and stared at me as I paddled silently near them. Just fifty yards away, I saw two sea otters, one lying on its back cracking a shell and the other in the process of diving. To my surprise the one on its back ignored me as I slowed the kayak to look at it. The calm shallow water and the partly sunny light enabled me to see clearly the reef underneath; sea weeds, sea urchins, sea stars, and a wealth of bivalves were seen in abundance. Sea otters should have no problem finding food here.

Yet, there is a major problem lurking in this beautiful rich coastal reef. It involves the triangle of people, sea otters and sea urchins.

In recent years there has been an increasing pressure of commercial, recreational, and traditional fisheries on inter-

A sea otter feeds close to John's Rock, Cap Flattery.

tidal marine invertebrates. The gonads of sea urchins are considered a delicacy and are intensively sought after by high end restaurants. This poses an immediate and serious threat to sea otters.

In fact, sea urchin populations are depleted in areas along the coasts which are shared by increasing densities of sea otters and fisheries, as is the case along the shoreline east of Neah Bay. When sea urchins and other sought-after invertebrates are hard to find, sea otters will move along the coastal reefs where kelp abounds, eager to find their favorite delight. Left to the natural forces along the coastal reef, the otters' dispersal pattern will follow the dynamics of food availability, filling new unexploited habitats nearby or far away.

A recent study of the sea otter in the Washington coast suggested just that. The population of fifty-nine individuals introduced in the 1970s has grown to merely eight hundreds in only four decades. Most likely, this population increase will continue until it reaches its optimal geographical range dependent on the availability of food.

However the direct competition for shared resources with people throws another unknown into the fray. Recent increased harvest activities for bivalves and other marine invertebrates along the Olympic Peninsula shores, on top of the feeding pressure of sea otters practically depleted sea urchins from these reefs. As a result, both human and sea otter populations end up losing their livelihood.

Another sea otter popped out of the water fifty yards away from my idled kayak and started to handle the food item it brought up. An old noisy fishing boat passed not far from my starboard slowly making good progress toward the open ocean. I rounded a set of large exposed rocks and ventured into a kelp bed, yo-yoing within a pond-like enclosure.

As I studied a kelp section where I heard a cracking sound of an otter feeding, I kept thinking about the otter and human relationship. Intense management of bivalves and sea urchins fishery within the kelp habitats is clearly needed. A recent study suggests rotational harvest schedules in the reef habitats which would maintain urchin population levels less likely to cause irreversible decline. That study further suggests encouraging management that emphasizes long-term viability of the kelp communities.

I believe that coexistence of humans and sea otters is possible if there is a trend toward optimizing fishery yields and at the same time maximizing preservation efforts of the natural habitat.

Sea otters could face disaster from another human activity—large or frequent oil spills from tankers which haul crude oil to the nearby refineries can easily exterminate sea otters. Sea otters have no blubber in their body. They rely on a layer of air trapped among the dense fibers of their fur

147

Waatch Point, the southern tip of Cape Flattery, and the rocks at the mouth of Waatch River.

for insulation against the cold ocean water and for buoyancy. A spilled oil layer on the otter's fur would be disastrous to its skin insulation. It would not be able to keep its core body temperature for long and it would perish from the cold. Can measures be taken to prevent oil spills?

Slowly I rounded Waatch Point, keeping the kayak off the surf, waiting for a good opportunity to enter the mouth of the Waatch River a hundred yards away. A few brown pelicans hovered low above me when I reached the soft flow of the incoming tide.

Hundreds of sea gulls fetching the surge that flashed the beach moved reluctantly south from the white sandy shoal where I landed.

It was now five hours since I settled in the kayak in Neah Bay. After a short rest I explored the first two miles of the Waatch River, and then returned to the ocean, past the breakers. I paddled leisurely within the swells of Makah Bay for a while enjoying the early afternoon hours before rolling the kayak to Hobuck Beach to my rented cabin.

148

Makah Bay, Olympic Coast. The Waatch River and the Sooes River which collect their waters from the western flanks of the Olympic Mountains empty to the Pacific Ocean here.

The next morning I launched into Makah Bay just as the fog faded off. It was an hour before low tide, and with the incoming breakers being weak I glided smoothly in the mild and cool wind to the open sea enjoying the soft ride on the beefy swells. The weather was predicted to stay mild today and I directed the kayak toward Anderson Point, about two miles to the south, negotiating my way between the exposed rocks carpeting the course.

A group of pelagic cormorants flying low toward the open ocean crossed my path. My plan today was to explore the coastline south of Makah Bay. This rugged coastline is part of the Olympic Coast National Marine Sanctuary. Looking east, I could see the Olympic Mountains still brushed with layers of fog, mainly at lower elevations and in ravines, in spite of the sun, and this gave the whole area an appearance of a green carpet of a temperate rainforest, adorning the mainland.

The weathered sea stacks in front of me were a spectacular sight with the many waterfowl dancing in, out, and around them. Cormorants, brown pelicans, and gulls perched on the exposed cliffs and rocks, kept taking off intermittently, to soar and then descend toward the water. The pelicans kept striking the water and then soared up again with their catch. As I approached one of the sea stacks at Anderson Point, the cormorants took off instantly while harlequin ducks grouped afloat in a protected shallow cove making soft whistle sounds.

The ocean along its coastline is quiet this morning. But most of the time it is not. Large swells collide mercilessly and incessantly with great force on the nearby exposed rocks and boulders with no intermissions, a very dangerous situation for any kind of vessel.

Solo sea kayaking here is probably not the wisest idea. Yet paddling alone within this magnificent natural setting, having all to myself the beauty and the spiritual tranquility of the motion of the swells and the sounds of their break, trumps my fear of the possible dangers. I'm focused and composed, and with all my senses tuned into the moment, I can hear all sounds and detect almost everything around me, noticing the minutest details.

Of course, familiarity with the ocean and its coastline behavior helps. The prognostics of marine weather forecasting, tide and current predictions, and swell height are easily available via internet links and through local knowledge. These make it easier to find windows of opportunity to paddle these ocean shores as long as one is prepared.

As I entered the protected cove I followed the harlequins and lingered a bit to observe these beautiful ducks intimately. A big mass of kelp blocked the way to the exposed reef. The harlequins were busy searching for food in the sea weeds loosely covering the reef where the surging water was washed off. This section was somewhat unprotected from the open ocean.

The ducks used a combination of swimming and wading techniques to negotiate these wet rocks. At times they walked on the reef like shorebirds, and at other times they either dabbled or dived into the deep. The harlequin ducks which prey on moving crustaceans, mollusks, and insects have learned to maximize their feeding efforts in these torrential waters along the Northwest coasts where they live year round.

Moving on I skirted the reef outside the surf, where I sighted three sea otters foraging in a tiny fjord, and then I rounded Portage Head and moved into a cove enclosed within sheer walled cliffs loaded with tide pools. It seemed I had entered a magical kingdom in a legendary land—sea gulls, pigeon guillemots, an oystercatcher, tufted puffins, auklets, and cormorants roamed the pools and deeper sections of

Sooes River Mouth at Makah Bay, Pacific Ocean.

the cove and five harbor seals were napping sprawled on a surge-free rock. What a diverse collection of marine fauna!

This reef enclosure is the northernmost tip of the spectacular Shai-Shai beach. I was tempted to land on the beach, but decided against it. Time was running late, and a strengthening southwest wind started to brush the surface of the sea, creating small ripples flickering over the five foot swells.

I turned the kayak north and pacing my paddle, headed back to Makah Bay into calmer waters. I rounded the large reef situated close to the entrance to Sooes River,

and glided on top of gentle surf into the mouth of the Sooes. High tide was moving in, deepening the narrow channel to the river. The white sandy shoals on each side of the river were filling up. The only sound that could be perceived was that of the small surge wavelets hitting the shore.

I landed on the north sandy beach for a short stretch, walking toward the open bay. As the incoming sea water moved further into the estuary, a group of vocal seagulls and a dozen brown pelicans moved in from the bay, leaving a nearby reef which was submerging under the incoming sea, and

150

Paddling the mouth of the Sooes River can be challenging at times.

landed, some along the shoals and some at the river mouth.

I located some dry heavy driftwood stems and sat comfortably on top of one. Gazing at the ocean, the incoming swells, the breakers, the surf washing the beach, the shorebirds running back and forth along the shoreline foraging on anything the incoming surge reveals, the few people walking on the vast beach scouting for treasures washed out from the ocean—I could not stay away from the idea that beneath this coastline, at this very moment of my silence, the oceanic crust is violently active.

The North American Plate is constantly drifting somewhat above the non-static Juan de Fuca Plate. Both plates are supported by an igneous active fluid layer that drags these two plates along. Any collision between the two plates is predicted to ignite the submerged tectonic canyons found five to seventy miles off shore. The immense energy created would sink coastline bluffs and boulders, would lift the inland terrain creating new relief, would rouse earthquakes that would send lava fluid into lowland ravines and rivers, and raise ocean swells to Tsunami magnitude.

This explosion can occur at any second between now and two hundred or more years from now, or be delayed even much longer. Looking at the horizon and the undulation of the ocean waves, the comings and goings of the waterfowl and the people, I find it hard to believe that permanence is just a deceiving illusion.

In the hope that such devastating catastrophe does not happen soon, what is important at the moment is to help preserve this ecologically rich coast in as much of its natural state as is possible, with the least human impact possible.

The chilling fact is that the stretch of this coastline and its offshore waters, from Cape Flattery in the north to the Columbia River in the south is governed by battalions of different federal, state, and local tribal entities, each with its own agendas, visions, and goals. These entities are all policed by human self interest, and more often than not emotionally motivated, and most likely lasting for only short-lived periods of time before new politics and interests emerge.

The swells were now breaking with explosive force and the sun was about to vanish into the horizon, brushing the sky with beautiful orange and pink illuminations. I put the kayak on the folding cart and slowly rolled it along the wet beach toward the cabin on Hobuck Beach. The silhouetted sea stacks and swells in the distance, the soaring gulls and cormorants flying to their night roosts, and the coming surge flushing my neoprene water shoes reminded me that the Olympic Coast is very much alive.

151

Getting ready to cut the breakers on the way to the open ocean.

12

Hoh River to Hoh Head

Landing safely.

It was mid morning with the fog lying low on the Hoh River when I launched at the south bank just outside the community of Hoh about two miles upstream from the river mouth. My plan was to float down to the river's mouth, enter the Pacific Ocean and explore the reef and the high cliffs of Jefferson Cove and Hoh Head two miles to the north. The visibility at the water line was fair and the current was unnoticeable. Ocean water should be coming in at the river opening by now. The next predicted high tide for the day was at quarter to four and I wanted to reenter the river just a little after the change of the tide.

The river meanders through a thick rainforest to the south where both sides of the channel are shallow and in places exposed. The thin fog blanketing the surrounding forest and its shrubby under-growth rolled just above the moving water giving this place a haunted atmosphere. A lone fisherman, in chilly weather gear flying bait upstream into the current nodded as I floated by. In the distance, on the south side of the river, I could see in vague outline, the tip of the spit that marked the river's mouth where I was heading.

The channel was now narrow, squeezed from both sides by the north and south

Brown pelicans and sea gulls cover the Hoh River narrow estuary.

154

lining spits. Hundreds of sea gulls and a great number of brown pelicans could be seen, some soaring above and some resting on the spits and the exposed shoal in the middle of the river.

The Hoh River originates high in the Olympic Mountains from the south flanks of the High Divide, the west slopes of Bailey Range, and from the Hoh, Blue, and White Glaciers of Mount Olympus. The river's two main forks cut abruptly through a dense and elaborate temperate old growth rainforest and channels its way out and in through the Olympic National Park to meet the Pacific Ocean just north of the First Nation's community of Hoh.

The river meanders through ancient lush flora of giant conifers such as Sitka spruce, western hemlock, western red cedar, and Douglas fir. Deciduous bigleaf maples decorated with lichens, mosses, and ferns dominate the canopy. About fourteen feet of rain are poured here annually by Pacific storms. In a world where hardly any area is left free from human encroachment, it is the largest untouched temperate productive rainforest.

Leaving the river's mouth I glided on a series of two-foot incoming swells which marked the entrance path to the ocean, paddled swiftly for another 200 yards into the open sea and then shifted north toward Hoh Head. Although the high tide inundated the river's mouth area for two hundred yards into the ocean, I was still in a shallow zone. The fog was hovering above the waters, but it appeared that the sun was

Approaching Hoh Head.

working its warmth to consume the mist. The rocks, the sea stacks, and the shoreline were easily visible now.

Less than fifty yards toward Jefferson Cove an exposed reef with a small cone-like sea stack, where a dozen brown pelicans were floating near the exploding small waves, caught my attention. The shallow place was turbulent and murky and most of the exposed rocks were covered with sand. I could not figure out what the pelicans were up to, but the sand-covered reef intrigued me for the evident powerful forces of erosion and sand deposit taking place here.

Immense ocean storms constantly hit the Olympic Peninsula lowlands and mountains, especially during late fall and through the winter. Condensed heavy clouds trapped at the western slopes of the Olympic Mountains release piles of snow and much rain for days on end. Excessive amounts of water move with power and force down the slopes and ravines dragging with them organic debris and eroded silt into the Hoh River to be deposited outside the river's mouth.

Evidence of the eroded earth can be seen along the river lowland course where many shoals and islets are spotted; this is why the mouth of the river is so narrow. The sand particles hurled into the ocean by the fast flow of the river, and by the forces of the tidal currents, constantly move northbound along the shoreline, and then as the waters

In a world where hardly any area is left free from human encroachment, the Olympic National Park is probably the largest untouched temperate productive rainforest.

hit the wall of Hoh Head in the north, they settle on the coastal floor. The pattern of deflection and the direction in which the sand-filled water moves is governed by the Coriolis Effect, the counterclockwise movement of the waters.

Hoh Head to the north, jutting out for almost a mile into the ocean, blocks the moving sand particles from moving further north along the coastline. Thus an extensive sandflat is created along this water path. These natural floods are not the only reason for land erosion affecting the Hoh watershed. The dense forest outside the park boundaries is constantly being thinned out by clear-cutting, opening the land to be broken by the forces of runoffs initiated by the pouring rains.

As I slide toward Jefferson Cove I make sure not to get close to the calm rugged shore which is too shallow, although the sheer bluffs towering the rocky beach are beautifully designed with ample holes and miniature caves. I could see two mature bald eagles perched side by side on a bare rock half way up the Head observing the breaking waves while a group of harlequin ducks, some puffins, and grebes busied themselves outside the surf near by.

As the sun finally speared through the remaining thin fog unveiling the Olympic foothills and lowlands, I turned my kayak around to return to the Hoh River, merging with the open ocean and cruising south which gave me a wide-angle view of the coastal foothills.

From this viewpoint I sadly eyeballed the numerous forest clearcuts scattered along these lowland areas extending from the Olympic National Park boundary all the way to about two miles from the coast, for about 40 miles.

A clearcut slope, where only a lean soil layer rests on bedrock, creates landslides caused by torrential rain, high winds, and frost with permanent loss of a vegetation cover. The extra eroded material, in turn, may dam streams, cover fish spawning sites, and bury available nutrients for stream fauna, effectively destroying riparian habitats. Besides losing natural old growth and forest soil, clear-cutting breaks the continuity of the greater Olympic watershed ecosystem with its diverse habitats and dynamic food webs. Even though timber management is using state of the art information on how to create least damage to the environment, I am struck again and again with how we think and act on a short term scale.

It was slack time now, following the tidal change which started less than an hour ago. I was just in time to enter the Hoh River

The coastline south of Mahah Bay is part of the Olympic Coast National Marine Sanctuary.

157

paddling easily through the deep narrow channel. The pelicans and the gulls were still where I had left them a while ago, and some were soaring now above my head.

Compared to the urbanization along the I-5 corridor, with its industrial and commercial entities, the Olympic Peninsula is a pristine dream. Presently, the Olympic National Park—including its lowlands, foothills, mountains, and the coastal shores—preserves the natural core of the diverse ecological systems which so many plant and animal species rely upon.

Slowly, enjoying my last moments at the lush old growth within the river's course, I landed on the gravelled public beach where my car was parked.

Can we steward our lands without sowing the grounds, waters, and air with toxins?

Above: To the east of the Interstate 5 urban corridor, rivers from the Northern Cascades hold ample precious clean waters and a diverse natural biota.

Below: To the west of the Interstate 5 urban corridor these clean waters become polluted leaving mostly toxic matter to reach the waters of Puget Sound and the Pacific Ocean.

Epilogue

These are the stories of my paddling voyages from the mountains of the Northern Cascades to the waters of the Pacific Ocean. I store with me many more stories and more memories to be kept to myself for the rest of my life. When I sea kayak alone, I'm in my zone; I'm transforming myself into the water that carries me along natural spaces that I cherish. I'm in a realm of solitude, freedom, and tranquility which are the essence of sea kayaking. I'm not the only one who felt this essence, talked, or wrote about it. Rivers of words were written by others describing it. I'm a continuum of this flow. Most people love and cherish nature. Most people have the urge to be in nature—alone or with friends, even for a short moment—to enjoy the warm sun, to watch the leafing of trees in the spring, to walk along a stream, to listen to the tunes of flowing water, to observe a bird, to encounter a deer, to climb an icy peak, or to stroll along a coastal beach feeling the surge tickle bare feet. We need these moments to get away from our daily routines.

Will we be able to continue to enjoy the mountains, the rivers, the wetlands, and the coastal waters without diminishing them? Will we learn to balance the use of our precious resources without overexploiting them? Will we be able to steward our lands without sowing the grounds, waters and air with toxins and pollutants?

Sea kayak and enjoy nature as long as it is still here.

Enjoy nature as long as it is still around.